As I Am:

Accepting Myself in An *Unacceptable* Society

Danielle Alyse

As I Am: Accepting Myself in an Unacceptable Society

As I Am: Accepting Myself in an Unacceptable Society

As I Am: Accepting Myself in an Unacceptable Society

Table of Contents

As I Am: Accepting Myself in an Unacceptable Society

As I Am: Accepting Myself in an Unacceptable Society

Introduction

Who actually reads this part anyway? Oh! You do, ha! Well, I'm hoping you do! I do as well, so I'm thinking that just maybe I'm not ACTUALLY alone in that. Well, let me put it this way, I don't read the introduction, rather it is the part I skim through to see if I want to read the book or not. Yeah, that's better worded, but I would guess most people share in that behavior.

Now that that's clear, this book is certainly one that I believe our world needs right now so I am anticipating that it will be a book that many read. Why? Because people are walking around so unhappy with their lives and many of them do not understand why or how they can shift that. So, I wrote this book for anyone interested in personal development, but really for the many out there that believe that they like themselves, but really do not TRULY accept or deeply love themselves.

As I Am: Accepting Myself in an Unacceptable Society

This book is for the ones who can only admit it on RARE occasions, because admitting this means we SHOULD take some form of action that generally equals us becoming uncomfortable. And, well, let's face it - NO ONE LIKES being uncomfortable, hence why only 1% of the world population is 'successful', right? Right. I heard it said by Natalee Hooper that "YOU HAVE TO BE comfortable being uncomfortable." This is the start of true growth.

So, forgive me in advance as I warn you that this book may possibly make you a lit-tle uncomfortable. Well, maybe I shouldn't have told you that, but if you're thinking of putting the book down, I would encourage you to at least get through this part first. See, I wrote this book for all those out there who know that they need just a smidge of help to change their lives but have no clue where to start. If you're not looking to change your life, chances are – then this book isn't for you. I'll tell you upfront that you have to start with accepting truth; even if that truth upsets you or makes you uncomfortable.

As I Am: Accepting Myself in an Unacceptable Society

I wrote this book for those who do love themselves, yet still find the tendency to be a "people pleaser" and all they need is a little nudge to become free from those tendencies. This book is intended to give people the perspective from my journey in order to show them they are not alone; in order to show them that a life filled with fulfillment, joy and happiness IS indeed attainable. This book is for those who have lost their way in life, or (honestly) maybe never really found it to begin with. It is intended to give insight, resources, ideas, alternate views, and finally – to ignite critical thinking; its purpose is to not only encourage but to challenge you, the reader, towards a positive, healthy view of SELF. This book is a map that is meant to guide you to the destination called, "My Best Life." I want you to know that "the good life" is NOT just meant for a certain set of people only – no, the "good life" is accessible to you as well!

This book also incorporates a few of my Christian beliefs because my faith is part of MY AUTHENTIC self. In sharing my beliefs, my intention is not to change what you believe, but it is to help you identify what you believe for yourself. I want people of any belief to read this, but it will be imperative to have an open mind to accept the views of others as their views, without taking ownership with those views if you desire not to. Being opened to hear the way someone else views the world is an important part of life development that I believe our society has lost. If we ever want to see change around us, then we must first willingly listen to how OTHERS interpret the world. This does not automatically mean... WAIT... This IS only the Introduction, right?! Dang, ok. Let's save this part of acceptance for a later chapter! I guess this is a good time to warn you that from time to time, I can totally go left on a topic when I was supposed to turn right! So, what was I saying? Oh! Yes!

My hope is that if you are reading this, or rather – SINCE you are reading this – then you are READY! "Ready for what?", you're probably thinking. Well, I hope you're ready for SOMETHING "TO GIVE" in your life!!!! Ready to be challenged in a positive way. Ready to be totally honest with yourself. Ready to take inventory of where you are mentally and emotionally so that you can achieve more of your life's goals. Ready to be open to the topics presented from my personal experiences, and ready to receive my viewpoint in order to gain a greater understanding of whether you actually need a book like this or simply if it's best to use this book to help others around you. Of course there are some that will not take interest in this book and may even judge it as something "not for them", and that's fine of course. However, in nearly 37 years of life, I have observed that it's those of us saying or thinking, "It's not for me," are the ones whom need this the most. OKAY!? I'M JUST SAYIN'!!

Don't be that person. Commit to your personal development. Commit to your growth. If you are not growing, you are dying; this is a fact of life. So now, before you dive into this book, since you've made it this far, I'm going to assume you've decided this is worth the read. So, I want to thank you for choosing YOU. I want to thank you for investing in you and taking the time, not to simply support this title, but to support your growth! I encourage you to read thoroughly and experience change from within along the way. It is my sincere hope that when you put this book down that you will be transformed into such a greater version of yourself! But don't stop there. No way, if your life changes from this book – require everyone you love to grow! Ultimately, it is the best for THEM so you're not trying to sell them a book – you're "selling" (if we want to use that word I guess) them a better version of themselves! Once you complete this book, I encourage you to take the initiative to share it with others. This is how things go viral and is how change can take place quickly! Imagine how much better the world would be if we all just "worked on ourselves" and then challenged others to be a better version of themselves, while of course embracing one another along the process.

Change always begins with looking at yourself first and then adjusting as need be – as the King of Pop once told us with his title, "Man in the Mirror."

Every word to that song hits the nail on the head! I honestly believe one of the biggest problems of today's world is that so many people are walking around secretly unhappy WITH THEMSELVES due to their own insecurities but and they project those feelings onto others. See the truth is - we cannot show or give what we do not first possess. If we do not possess self-love and acceptance, how can we give it. This is why change starts in the mirror! Unfortunately, this is causing majority of people to live a life of suffering because our society doesn't focus on emotional wellbeing as much as we need it to.

Well, it is the 21st century people! We HAVE TO GET A GRIP and that's exactly what this book is designed to do - catch that grip. It's meant to discuss how important true self-acceptance and love is, and how drastically dehydrated our culture is of these two. This book will help us understand the benefits of FULLY accepting one's WHOLE SELF, JUST AS THEY ARE....

So, in a nutshell I've explained how important this book is to me for the use of personal development. I would also like to share with you another type of people I'm looking for as the perfect reader to this title. Over the years, I have also found that lots of people struggle with their attention spans and are desperately seeking to improve their quality of life in this area (our society doesn't help this factor either, of course). This is especially evident when it comes to reading; there is just something about deep topics where there are no dragons breathing fire, no romance being kindled, or no murder mysteries to solve that simply zaps the interest right from some readers, no matter how interested they are in the book. So I wanted to make this book attention keeping. No, I needed to make this book interactive. See, I have discovered that I have a superpower known as ADD/ADHD. What that means is that I get easily distracted all the time, like recording breaking minutes (great, huh!?) – even with the help of medicine and many tools in my tool belt to help. If you have that superpower too, ha! you'll discover throughout these pages doodle places, note taking lines, and even physical things to do – thus allowing yourself permission to set the book down without feeling guilty. (I used to feel guilty when I would read a book I knew could or was helping me, but I just got too bored to finish it.) I knew that in writing this book that it would need to be interactive, so that you would be able to follow along while staying engaged. At the same time there are usually multilevel meanings for the way I do things. Strategic is another fun word to use, I guess. Ha! Yes, Ok. I do things strategically to achieve multiple things simultaneously.

While I want you to remain engaged during reading this title, I want to also cultivate an atmosphere in your mind that will make intentional thinking attainable. Intentional on what? Well, I hope that through my own story you will believe that your life can be different. I want you to believe that you CAN absolutely stop any life cycle that seem so unbreakable. So I want to create intentional dialogue in her mind for a life of victory! See, I don't know if you'll be able to relate but for years, I would find myself ending up at the same place in life; I wasn't out there making a ton of poor decisions to lead me there. I would make positive changes, yet it always seemed as if I was just doomed to continue the cycles that kept me stuck in life. I would get on my feet financially and be trucking along only to hit a pothole or 5! It was never just be a bump in the road either, it would be like one thing after the other that threw all my progress out the window. What's that saying? When it rains it pours! Yes, that was my life. It was literally to the point that I could predict the chain events when they started to happen, and of course they would come as I predicted.

It was a series of life events that hit me all at once and knocked me to what I felt was my absolute bottom. It was in this moment I finally saw that I could actually put a halt to the vicious cycle I deemed and accepted as my life's story. I want to add just a little thought here though (because I'll share more on this later) - the events that led me to the place I needed to be, which prompted the internal changes, did not stop hitting me just because I decided to change my perception and claim victory. No, instead what I found was an increasingly profound amount of new strength and a new attitude to face the next year, leaving behind the initial life shattering events in the past.

Things often get worse before they get better and maybe you're reading this book in your season of "worse"; I want to encourage you that you've opted to read the right book in the right season of your life. Truthfully, if I had never experienced my season of extreme pressure, this book could not have been birthed. The best is worth the hard work to get to it. It's the same with such the finer things in life like gold and diamonds. A diamond is a simple piece of coal; it needs to be exposed to extreme heat and pressure before it can shine and transform into the most precious stone that we know it as.... Such is life, and such are you and I.

Read this book with the understanding that I want to motivate people (you) to think intentionally. My goal is to challenge others to step outside their normal view of life in order to catch a glimmer of the possibilities. Possibilities of abundant life, of living out their dreams, of being able to wake up every day thankful, to not have to hide behind fake smiles or live with self-destructive behaviors a single day more. I want to inspire others to evaluate their thoughts and feel capable of changing them; understanding that in doing so it will change their lives. I want others to take back control of their mental health and their emotional being, so that they can genuinely live a life that they once only dreamed of. I pray my words can manifest the power that I know is within each and every one of us; the ability to create the world we individually live in to be one of abundance and beauty. It starts within yourself. You see, you must get to a place where like I, you accept your whole self. The good, the bad, the ugly, and all the in between.

So, what exactly do I want you and all others to take away from this book? When you complete this book, I want you to:

- ✓ Feel compelled to evaluate your "I Am" perspective.
- ✓ Be motivated and inspired to evaluate your personal belief systems and your values.

As I Am: Accepting Myself in an Unacceptable Society

- ✓ Cultivate a tribe of people, a community of self-love; for when you accept, you can truly love.

- ✓ Be educated in a new area.

- ✓ Feel a stir from the inside so that you are moved to action.

- ✓ Know that you can change the world by changing yourself

As you're reading this book, I want you to FEEL:

- ✓ Challenged

- ✓ Accepted (by me and you!)

- ✓ Not alone

- ✓ Encouraged

- ✓ Motivated

- ✓ Courageous- (like the cowardly lion at the end of the Wizard of Oz you know?!)

- ✓ Willing

- ✓ Some sadness and anger but in the sense that you see you have been living beneath your capacity

- ✓ Awakened

- ✓ Forgiving towards themselves

As I Am: Accepting Myself in an Unacceptable Society

- ✓ Informed

- ✓ Significant (not prideful)

- ✓ Uncertain, but trusting

- ✓ Prepared to take action and move forward even on the days that are challenging

- ✓ Better equipped for life's trials and journey

- ✓ Empowered to make positive and lasting changes for their individual lives.

- ✓ Supported, not coddled

- ✓ Inspired

- ✓ Excitement at the journey of self – discovery

Ultimately, I hope you begin to find that you can trust yourself and your higher power, once you get to a place where you can accept yourself wholly. This in turn will help you walk through uncertainty with trust in yourself and in God or your higher power. This book's purpose is to minister to the spirit man of each reader, awakening the power within and allowing that power to manifest each one's gifts, talents, and purpose.

As I Am: Accepting Myself in an Unacceptable Society

My purpose for this book is to help you realize that coming to genuine truth within yourself is the most freeing thing that you could ever do. That allowing yourself to face some ugly things about yourself head on, releases emotional blocks which will change the course of your life. When we believe different about our lives, about OURSELVES, then things begin to look different. When we can change the way we think, we can change our life. It must start with ourselves, as cliché as that sounds. Michael Jackson had it right y'all, it starts with the man in the mirror. Take a break, listen to it, and allow the lyrics to penetrate your spirit and soul. Here's a quick suggestion, feel free to YouTube that song and dance around for a few minutes to it. Or you can just listen to it - that's fine too, but the key is, those words are powerful. So, just take a break to enjoy the moment, and come back for the official beginning of this title, "Here I Am."

As I Am: Accepting Myself in an Unacceptable Society

Here I Am.

So, here we are. Look at that! We made it through the first chapter. Want to know something interesting? If you thought that Introduction section was long, it was waaaaaaay longer! HA! Bet you're as grateful for my editor as I am! So. Here we are, and here I am. Let's dive into this.

"True belonging is the spiritual practice of believing in and belonging to yourself so deeply that you can share your most authentic self with the world and find sacredness alone in the wilderness. True belonging doesn't require you to change who you are, it requires you to be who you are" (Brene Brown, Braving the Wilderness pg. 40).1

I love how the author states, "True belonging doesn't require you to change who you are, it requires you to be who you are," because over the course of my life's journey I spent more time attempting to change who I was. I would have these thoughts that if I could just change this about myself, or if I did that differently life would be better for me. The

As I Am: Accepting Myself in an Unacceptable Society

list got exhausted with statements that revolved around if I could change or if I would just do differently then my life would surely be what it is supposed to be. I never really felt like I belonged in any specific or set place, and I just knew I needed to change myself in order to do so. To others this did not seem like truth because I was always busy with something. Since I was a child, I had several diverse groups of friends I hung around. Sometimes a few individuals intertwined with a couple of the groups, but this was mostly because I never seemed to fit in one group. As an adult I got involved in church shortly after my son was born and this narrowed my groups down. I still always felt like an outsider, or at least the one who did not fit completely. When I was younger it didn't bother me as much because to me, I just saw it as being eclectic and that I just needed variety in my life. That is still very much true, but as I hit my 30's I noticed that not belonging always left me feeling a little sadder deep within myself, and that I just masked it with my business over the years.

I was usually very liked by most who I encountered, but still very different than most of the people I was around. For years I thought I didn't belong because I came from the east coast and that's a much different culture than north Texas. I also grew up in larger towns, and for most of my beginning adult years I lived in an extremely small town. You don't always pay attention to how much you fit anywhere when you keep yourself going non-stop. It's the moments life causes you to stop when that feeling can no longer be kept hidden. It will consume some of us rather quickly when we've suppressed it for so long. The picture that comes to mind is a small trash can at a car mechanic shop, full of dirty rags that has been saturated with gasoline. I mean, all you have to do is just barely make a spark, and POOF! The rags instantly disintegrate into flames. Things in my life just seemed to work in the opposite flow from most others around me. I wouldn't say I had "bad luck", but I will say, definitely, weird crap would find its way to haunt me. It was always as if I did things backwards when compared to others. I also have learned by now that comparing ourselves to others does us zero justice and is something that I highly guard myself from doing these days. I mean, if you take the time to look at all the facts comparing ourselves to others does not make logical sense. Let me give you one of the best examples I personally have.

As I Am: Accepting Myself in an Unacceptable Society

I became pregnant with my son at age 17. It was the end of my junior year in high school, and he was born right at one month after my 18th birthday, in the middle of what should have been my senior year. I did marry his father, but we also divorced quickly, and I was a single mother for just about all his life. There are plenty of other single mothers out there who had their kids at the same age as I and have extremely similar experiences. However, there are so many other factors that play into raising a child and trying to finish growing up yourself to even remotely compare myself to any other person who has a shared story. The support system one has is important along with other factors such as - do they have blood family around, what are the grandparents like, are they close by, are they involved, did the mother finish school or get some form of trade/career, does the father of the child pay child support even if he isn't present, is the father present, where do they live, what's the economic system like there, are there any health issues present in the mother or child, etc.? I mean the list could seriously go on and on. How each of these factors are answered truly separates this person's situation from mine. Even one of these factors can significantly change how we both as single teenage mothers end up being in the long run or the bigger picture. So much so that to compare we would have to have the same circumstances with the same upbringing ourselves and even more the same brains.

On top of all those external contributing factors, you have to consider how each of us were raised, and what our life & processing skills are. You would have to consider how both individuals "deal" with life. Even identical twins raised in the same home are going to grow up perceiving life slightly different than each other, and their own processing and life skills will develop uniquely. There are no two people who are that identical, we are all very unique. So tell me how comparing ourselves to another makes any logical sense when you take time to evaluate all the actual contributing factors? It doesn't. Yet, almost everyone I know, including myself, struggles so strongly with being quick to look around and think that we are less than or better than those sharing in one or two similar circumstances as us. It's come to my understanding that it is just as if I was going to compare the way a potato grows to the way reptiles reproduce. Or apples to oranges if you prefer, but it's still comparing fruit. Nevertheless you still get very different end results, even if you give both the exact same care. At the end of the dad-gum day you would still have apples versus oranges, two significantly different types of fruit!

I said all of that to show you how silly it is when we constantly judge ourselves or our lives based on comparisons. This is so damaging to our own self view, and it distorts the way that we see others as well. Most of the time when we compare, we end up making untrue conclusions about those we are comparing ourselves to. Not only have we devalued ourselves, but we have excessively elevated others. When we elevate others, it is damaging because by doing so, we place those people on pedestals; and trust me they will fall off. Comparison is a thief that robs us of joy, peace, and fulfillment; not to mention that it is emotionally draining. I mean come one, I am already emotionally worn out just explaining this all to you! Let's take a mind break, why don't we?

As I Am: Accepting Myself in an Unacceptable Society

Calming, huh? Now, moving on...

It took me 36 years and going through a second divorce (among a few other life changing events that I will elaborate on later) to finally learn that I never truly belonged anywhere because I did not first belong to myself. For whatever reason I never wholeheartedly learned to love myself, to totally accept myself; good, bad, and all my in between - as I was just because I was me. There were times I got very close to doing so, and I would begin to be my authentic self, only to allow the words (even from the past) of others and my own insecurities to force me back into the rejection cycle. I would feel as if my differences were too much for others to accept. I would allow myself to dwell on that so much that it led me to believe I wasn't enough or either I was really just TOO MUCH. That led me to turning back into the chameleon, to be like whomever I was around the most or whomever I put on the highest pedestal. I would let enough of my true self come out to stand out and be seen, but the very second, I felt the tiniest sense of rejection or as if I didn't fit or belong - I would abandon those things about myself that made me unique. There were also times that I over amplified those unique traits too, but that was just the obnoxious attempt to overcompensate so I could belong. I can remember thinking, "Well if I really am THAT different in this area than surely, I will at least belong to the misfits group" or whatever group I categorized in that season of my life. It was chaotic and created such a drama cycle that I never even understood, let alone saw it as it was.

Alright, so what finally changed? Life. Ha! As if the first divorce wasn't enough - I found myself going through another divorce. Let me say, no time in life is ever the "perfect" time for a divorce but this one happened at a very difficult time in any woman's life who is a mother; my only son had recently graduated from high school during this time. Moms, I didn't even have an empty nest yet, but there was just something about the idea of my only son graduating that hit me in a way that I never expected it to do.

I mean, all I had known for the past 18 years revolved around caring for him. Of course, I still am doing so (to an extent), just in a much different way than before but truthfully, that was a difficult transition. Another thing that happened during the time of this divorce was our church closed. When it did, I realized that I had mostly hid from my own inner self behind the church. "Find another church," you say; well, I did that. But you see - I come to the reality that my commitment to volunteering had become unhealthy over the years. I had known for several years leading up to this church closure that I needed to re-evaluate the area of my relationship with God and the balance with church serving. I knew I needed this break, but what I didn't expect was it to come during the same time I would be going through a divorce, or my son would be out of high school.

Even worse, I also realized during this time that for most of the years raising my son I was literally always going to college and then bam, suddenly, I was free. Like, I was divorced and free. I was "empty nest" and free. I was "volunteer-less" and free. And now, go figure - I was "time free." I wasn't "money free" though! HA! I had reached my maximum amount to borrow for student loans, so it made double sense to take simply take a short break. Well, I had three semesters left to FINALLY get my Bachelors degree when I decided that break was good, and then the divorce happened. I knew my finances would not allow for me to go back and finish anytime soon.

It was halfway through my 35th year of my life, and all that I had known for the past 17 years at that time was coming to a major change. Now the marriage that was ending had only been part of the equation for a little over a year, two years if you count the time we dated. However, I had spent most of our engagement adjusting myself to this new family that I would have. I had poured everything into the marriage, and into the little guy that became my stepson, because I believed it was God's answer to life. It was just another distraction from my own inner self.

That divorce felt like it ripped my entire belief system, and all that I had ever known out from under me. I had poured so much into it, but little did I know then that it was the best thing that could have ever happened FOR me (not TO me). It forced me to focus on me, nothing nor anyone else. It forced me to accept the things I just had refused to deal with in the past. It forced me to dig deep within and ask myself so many questions I had never asked before; and then, most importantly - I also had to answer those questions. It made me question God, and everything I ever thought I believed, along with the values and the general belief systems I had been living by. It finally forced me to see myself for once.

I had always been self-reflective, and psychology is what I have studied in college. It has always been one of my life's passions, and as long as I can remember I thought I worked on myself to my very best in every season of my life. I, of all people, should have understood how important self-acceptance and self love was. It was through this relationship that ended abruptly that I realized I had not even truly scratched the surface of what it TRULY meant to accept myself, let alone completely love myself - the good, the bad, the confused, the ugly, the quirky, the very different in between parts of me. I was at my own rock bottom. I had to find out what I believed. I knew that God loved me enough to die for me, that Jesus literally sacrificed Himself and went through physical hell for my salvation and reconnection to God; but I found out during this season that I did not actually understand that. I could not fully understand that until I learned to look at myself without judgment and without comparing myself. I had to see myself as God saw me. My understanding is that because of Jesus dying on the cross and being the ultimate sacrifice for humans, when we accept that - ask Him (Jesus) to come live in our hearts and confess to Him that we are sinners who need help - we can then be reconnected with our true self, our God designed selves. So when God looks at me, He sees Jesus, His sinless child. When God looks at me, He sees me perfect and whole. No matter how many years I spent studying the bible, or serving and attending church, this concept was still so far from my true understanding. How could God see me perfect when I was such a stinking mess?!

But that's just it, walking according to faith, (whatever yours may be) isn't about what you do or what you have done. It isn't about how much of a mess you are either. Rather, it's about trusting in a greater being than yourself, and believing in what you don't or can't see. Faith, in any belief, is not ever about what we already THINK we know, it's about believing and trusting beyond our finite comprehension. Like I have said, I do consider myself of Christian faith, however I do not believe that I fit the "mold" that society has created. (That being said, I hope that you will continue reading with an open heart and a willing mind.)

As I Am: Accepting Myself in an Unacceptable Society

But see, it was during this rock bottom place in my life that I found out God wasn't exactly who I tended to think He was, and I wasn't the person I thought I was. Both things were pivotal for me, and yet so hard to adjust to. You see, we can believe something, but if we don't value it then we aren't really believing. And it's only when we value people or even things for that matter, that we begin to completely take care of those people and things.

For me, like many others, I honestly did not SEE or feel my own self value. I believed in God and what I was taught by spiritual leaders. I believed what the Bible said. I even had moments when I felt the most blissful, amazingly beautiful sense of peace, love, and joy - which I knew could only come from a being greater than me or of this world. However, I did not see God's value, because I could not see my own value. You see, when God created humans, in my mind, He created them as an extension of Himself. The Bible and most religious teachings say that God created humans to fellowship with him. He wanted to hang out with them and have best friends for life, eternity. So in my mind, and apparently in the minds of the scientist that confirm this, God is in our very DNA.

Because I am who I am, I spent several minutes, hours, and days attempting to understand my connection between my Creator and myself. What I came to was a profound conclusion that unless you understand the very nature of God, you will not understand your nature - since we are made in His image. For additional reading, I've added a few resources that have tied together for me what Jesus taught.

[The Power of I Am by Sharon and David Allen]

[The Divine MATRIX by Gregg Braden]

I will warn you that some of it may seem a little out there, as they are considered metaphysical and could be confusing to you. So please understand that my whole point is that God is part of each and every one of us no matter what belief about Him we hold. The most important advice that I would offer is to ask God to open the eyes of your understanding, to open your spiritual eyes. I would never want to confuse anyone, so I also would like to suggest if you struggle with your own beliefs about God that you find someone you can talk to. That someone should be one that you can trust and share openly with so that you can sort out for yourself what you believe, and not just what I or anyone else TELLS you to believe. However, this is not a book to tell you how or what kind of faith you should have. This is a book to share my journey of accepting myself in an unacceptable world, and part of accepting myself (as I have stated) includes my faith. My hope is simply as I share my life, that it will give you a new perspective in your life, and more importantly new eyes to see yourself with.

Before we get into deeper topics, I would like to warn you of one more thing. This book is unconventional, and it is going to contain some interactive areas throughout its pages. If you are going to take the journey with me towards learning how to accept yourself on a more authentic and genuine level, it is imperative that you have a sense of awareness of who I am without having to physically know me. I am a tad of an over processor, and my brain thinks about a million and one things at one precise minute; I have what is considered a very ADD/ADHD mind. I personally do not see this as a disease or disorder, although it has not always been the blessing I view it as now.

As I Am: Accepting Myself in an Unacceptable Society

Because of this, one of the things I wanted to be sure of when I wrote a book was that it had to have the power to appeal to those I knew would struggle to read it in its entirety. If that isn't you feel free to skip those pages, but you may just find yourself enjoying the little doodle places, and the word searches randomly placed within the pages.

In regard to my having an ADD brain, I know there are lots of controversial opinions about this along with other mental health topics. This one is widely under and over diagnosed, and too often wrongly treated. As a result many people have a very distorted view of this term, and I would like you to, again, stay open minded and hear me out. I promise this is all very relevant in getting the most out of this book. I have seen ADD used as an excuse, but it truly is a thing. I heard it best described by a wonderful young lady who I watch from time to time that "it's like having 25+ televisions on in front of you, all with different shows on and you are trying to keep up and efficiently follow every one of them at the exact same time." ADHD does not have a one size fits all symptoms check sheet either, so just because you have some idea of what is and what isn't ADHD, please know you may be wrong. Keep in mind that people who suffer with blood pressure issues or diabetes do not all have the exact same list of symptoms. I have a list of all the sources I used to complete this book, and there will be some very helpful resources for this topic as well as others addressed. I will interchange ADD and ADHD so just be aware for me it means the same diagnoses, and for me it is the way my brain works.

I no longer believe that this is a disorder or disease or even an illness. It is something that some people can manage better than others, and it is something that adds variety to this turning world we know as our lives. I also believe that it is extremely important how we word things (and I will talk more about that later) so with that being said, I wanted to explain why I do not call this a "disorder" I have. I also do not like taking on the status quo so let's remember that and be quicker to tell yourself not to judge as you read, because you more than likely will. I mean come on, I wrote the book and I had to constantly stop and say out loud to myself, "Danielle - do not judge that, do not assume you know everything about anything. Danielle - let people discover for themselves and do not be so quick to over explain every little detail."

As I Am: Accepting Myself in an Unacceptable Society

We are human, and we live in a society where 24/7 we are faced with how, what, when, and why we are to think and believe whatever we are told. We live in a world shaped by nonrealistic expectations and false realities that we call social media and reality T.V. We are continuously bombarded with ideas and beliefs that we often do not even realize we soak in, until we begin calling them our own - only to find out we do not even know when exactly it was we adopted these ways and beliefs, and even much less why we did!

We live in a world that ties us to electronics, which we want to believe are giving us all these conveniences when really, it's only pushing us farther away from social skills. These devices have so much power to isolate us that they are only creating more division among each other and pushing us into forgetting ourselves along the way as well.

Ok, so please take note that I am not against technology or electronics, I am simply stating that this is the world we live in. I am stating that balance has been lost for some time now and unless we start calling it as it is, and choosing to take some action about it, we will end up much more lost - much faster than we have already seen. We must find that balance again. Balance. Life as we know it needs balance, and you cannot access your balance when your foundation isn't solid. I am going to say this - you can be the fullest of faith person trusting completely in God always - but if you worry, talk negative about yourself, act out of a place of false guilt and etc., then you are missing something! You are missing the very fact that God sees you a way you do not see yourself. Period.

Interaction Time...

After this sentence put the book down and do any form of whole-body physical activity.

- Jumping jacks.

- Stretches.

- Arm & Leg Lifts

MOVE YOUR BODY in some way physically...

Then...

Write down the date you started this book or today's date.

As I Am: Accepting Myself in an Unacceptable Society

Write one reason this book intrigued you.

Write one reason you felt lead to buy this book.

Write down one thing you hope to gain from this book!

As I Am: Accepting Myself in an Unacceptable Society

Date _____

_____

_____

_____

_____

_____

_____

_____

_____

_____

_____

_____

_____

_____

_____

_____

_____

_____

_____

_____

_____

_____

_____

_____

_____

_____

_____

_____

_____

_____

_____

_____

_____

_____

_____

_____

_____

_____

_____

_____

_____

_____

_____

_____

As I Am: Accepting Myself in an Unacceptable Society

Denial

Denial is one of those silent killers. It seeps deep inside and rots out the very root system of people, in my opinion. It is deception at its finest, and most of us walk around everyday wearing it like our favorite t-shirt. When we choose denial, we walk around believing lies that we have fabricated ourselves from within. I'm telling you - it's so darn sneaky! The reason we fight so hard to continue in denial is because we simply cannot believe we would be so deceived. I've heard it said that deception wouldn't be deception if we could see it! Many times we truly don't see that we're in denial because we don't want to; and then sometimes we know we are deceiving ourselves, but the lie just tastes much better! After all, no one wants to feel like a "fool", and let's be real for a minute, usually the reason for denial is going to be 1 of 2 reasons; 1- we don't want to take the responsibility that we need to take if we admitted the truth, or 2- we don't want to LOOK stupid, ignorant, or like someone "got one over" on us. Ultimately, the root connected to this lies in how we want others to perceive us and the fear of being rejected if being perceived the wrong way! Do you see how this will tie in with being 100% yourself and how deep the root of the denial will affect you?

Hear me say, this is NOT always intentional or even consciously done. Often, denial is something we have subconsciously learned as a defense mechanism, and most people honestly do not see that they are living in it. Often, we have that "inkling" inside telling us that something must change, but we do not want to believe the voice of our inner truth because we want to stay comfortable. (Although really, we're just comfortably uncomfortable.) We have adjusted well to life, and to see the truth about an internal trait, a person we love, or a thing we don't want to let go of would each require us to change. It would mean that we must adjust anything else that is related to either that trait, person or thing; whatever it is we are in denial about is a continual reminder that WE DO NOT LIKE CHANGE. Instead of rejecting denial and embracing change, many of us simply remain comfortable as we are; we would rather believe that we just don't "adjust well" and therefore change is not an option for us.

As I Am: Accepting Myself in an Unacceptable Society

Well, of course we don't adjust well when we continue to tell ourselves (and others) that we don't. Really, it is an excuse, but we proclaim it so often that we believe it. We will get more into how that whole speaking and believing things works as we get deeper in this book but as for denial, I will share that sometimes I felt completely disgusted with myself just thinking of how I thought I was so above many of the traits I clearly possessed! I couldn't believe how much denial I personally lived in for years. Yet, I was only able to truly see that once I started putting this book together. I saw pieces of my life shattered right before me that I thought were the strongest areas. I was wrong. I found as I was writing this book that I had been so wrong about the place I was in. As I wrote each page, then typed each section, I realized why my life was where it was; I felt angry, yet thankful, to finally be able to make some true progress. Despite how shocking this was to me, and how angry with myself I would get with every new realization, excitement welled up in me also! It was this excitement that fueled me to KEEP MOVING FORWARD during those terrifying moments in which I had to realize just how blinded I had been. This excitement fueled me every time I wanted to QUIT because it was INSANELY UNCOMFORTABLE. I was excited to allow these areas that had been stuck to become loose! I was excited to see what my life would be like after the process of healing, and in writing this book, I realized that I could SERIOUSLY do that; I could finally heal!

See, denial is that thing that keeps us from having to take assertive action about something. It's that "way out" in our minds, our way to hide from dealing with something we believe (or think) is going to be too difficult to handle. But that's just it, the very thing we believe denial does in itself is a lie. Denial deceives us into believing it will protect us from the pain, while all it does is increase the pain that we have and amplifies it. Denial creates a domino effect of false realities and negative emotions.

I will use myself as an example again. Let's use the trait that I talk excessively; and yes, I can honestly be talkative. But let's say I talk so much that I do not listen to others at all and they never can share anything with me due to my excessive talking .(The movie, "A Thousand Words" with Eddie Murphy is a great example of this, and I would certainly recommend you that you watch it sometime while reading this.) If I were to deny this were true, that is the first domino tile standing up, right? Okay, so since I am denying this trait about myself, over time those people will just talk to me less and less. At first, I may not even notice how little they are talking to me because I'm essentially wrapped up in myself talking. However, as time passes, I do notice that they are talking to me lesser, (and then because I am still denying my extreme talking), I start thinking of reasons why people talk to me less. BUT - wait - I do not ask these people of course, because doing that would mean what? It would mean facing something I MIGHT not really want to. Alternatively, let's just say that I do bring it up and instead of them giving me the truth - they protect my feelings (or maybe coward from their own) and don't give me the truth as I need to hear it.

Even worse, they add fuel to the fire by telling me that they've just been busy. Of course, that's fine but fast forward, I notice that they are super active on social media WITH other people! Or, I hear through the grapevine about their new adventure - one that has been shared with others, but not me! It now, of course, will dawn on me to wonder why they are making time for others but not me. THIS is when the fabricating begins. I begin to fabricate reasons or excuses as to why these people are not sharing their lives with me anymore! More than likely, I will feel rejected and because I feel rejected, I will become resentful and bitter.

In that one situation, denial produced rejection, resentment, and bitterness. I mean, and well...can I just call it like it is? Denial is basically lying. It's just a slightly fancier name. Most people will agree that when someone starts lying, that person generally tells more lies to cover up the last one, which is the same concept of the domino effect. This is what happens when you add more and more negative dominoes behind that first "denial domino." Each new thing added is another domino tile that we don't realize is in place and ready to fall at the very tip of the first one! Just as with the domino effect, denial and his family) is SERIOUSLY affecting the emotions of every other area in our lives. The more important thing to note: It only takes the smallest movement or wind to blow - pushing that first domino over and knocking all the rest down (In the movie Collateral Beauty, Will Smith's character is seen lining up dominoes).

As I Am: Accepting Myself in an Unacceptable Society

And we wonder why we have so many people suffering with mental illness. NIP IT IN THE BUD! Do not let yourself put up the first denial domino! If you have, it's okay! Now, you just need to give yourself permission to take it down along with any dominoes that follow. The only way we can do that is by being vulnerable and transparent. We must be willing to see it or evaluate it if someone else we trust lets us know that we are in denial in any measure. Again, denial is not just a river in Egypt! It is a serious authentic blocker! *Ha! You laughed, I bet ya!*

Denial is one of those words we hear and use, yet I wonder how many of us live everyday holding it in our hands. We make jokes about being fake, teasing others and carelessly tossing this word around. However, if we stopped to really think about it, are there areas within that we choose to live in a sense of denial about? Are there parts of our past or maybe certain tendencies we know we have that we don't like to talk about or admit to? If so, are we just keeping quiet about those things or are we straight up in some form of denial about whatever it may be?

As I Am: Accepting Myself in an Unacceptable Society

The Merriam-Webster dictionary says denial is "the refusal to admit the truth or reality of something, or the refusal to acknowledge a person or thing." It also says, "it is a psychological defense mechanism in which confrontation with a personal problem or with reality is avoided by denying the existence of the problem or reality." We all have traits that we wish weren't there, and baggage from life. Negative patterns and mindsets result from not knowing how to deal with dysfunction, or hard times during our life in a healthy way. Sometimes we are raised with certain negative mindsets or patterns, and we aren't even aware that these patterns are adding to our current struggles in life.

Just because we were raised with these denial patterns does not mean that we must continue in them. Again though, if we aren't willing to see them within ourselves, then we cannot change them. This is one of the many reasons people seem to stay stuck or repeating "family" history. We tend to hang out in this little realm called denial and too many people laugh it off like it's funny! We are COMFORTABLE. We know how to manage our dysfunction, and we too often justify to ourselves giving every reason known to mankind as to why IT'S REALLY OKAY.

No one ever wants to admit that they are spoiled, or they tend to be self-centered - wanting to get their way over someone else's more times than not. No one wants to believe that they default to using guilt trips on those around them. No one wants to believe they have a victim mentality or poverty mentality or whatever else negative mentality we all have heard of. No one THINKS that they manipulate others in order to control the world revolving around them or attempt to keep themselves from getting hurt. We can all read statements like this and our first thought is usually, "I agree with this, but this isn't me."

BE HONEST. REALLY HONEST...

So I am going to ask you to stop and think about this for a moment. Remember why you decided to read this book. This book is about accepting yourself in an unacceptable society. Alright, so there is no one around right now. It is you and this book. Hopefully you took my advice to get a journal. Take out the journal. I want you to answer these questions:

As I Am: Accepting Myself in an Unacceptable Society

Are you honestly wanting to learn how to fully accept and love yourself on a deeper level so that you can enjoy life in abundance?

_____

_____

_____

_____

_____

_____

_____

_____

_____

Do you SERIOUSLY want to learn more about yourself so that you can stop getting stressed out easily? So you can have a life full of joy and peace?

_____

_____

_____

_____

_____

_____

_____

_____

_____

Then the first thing you have to be willing to do is realize that there are probably things about yourself you might not like or worse, WANT to admit; listen, THAT IS OKAY! Admitting whatever it is does not mean those things get to have power over you. Nor do they define you as a person! We must FIRST accept EVERYTHING about ourselves! Be willing, open to see it all in a non-judging way before we can ever move into having a fully abundant life. We have got to be willing to take off our rose-colored glasses with ourselves. This is the foundation folks. Have you ever thought, "I don't do THAT, do I?" What about being in the middle of a conversation about one topic, and suddenly you're defending yourself over the topic when the person was not even talking about YOU and even stated that they weren't!? Yep!! We have a problem. You felt compelled to defend because YOU PROBABLY are living in a state of denial about something related to the topic! See our subconscious has this funny way of acting out in ways that we think "Where is that COMING from?" Well, it's coming from within YOU. It's coming from an area you may be choosing denial over instead of actual TRUTH.

What is so amazing is that once we do really get past our own denials, and face some things about ourselves, other people will not be able to use those things against us. Acknowledging is the first key to unlocking the unspoken prison denial keeps us bound in. Power is lost simply by acknowledging. Hence why, not only the Bible, but most all spiritual beliefs talk about confession. And here we all keep thinking it's about us airing our dirty laundry out for all to see. HA!

I told you a little bit about how I grew up, or well maybe I didn't but anyway. I was an only child. The truth is that growing up as an only child, you do not have to constantly share with siblings, so we do tend to be a little less aware of those around us. Even if we weren't spoiled with material things, we still never had to share at home. We did not have to share the attention of our parents either. For me, even with cousins around, I grew up less aware of others. I also grew up not being shown healthy coping skills, and I learned early on how to manipulate others with words - kind, nice, pleasant words. I honestly had no idea I used words to manipulate. I wasn't manipulating people directly, but what I would do was manipulate the things I said to people so then it would make people feel some kind of way, and they would end up doing what I wanted them to do. For example...

Let's say I was talking to someone I knew could watch my son so that I could go out without him. Instead of just directly asking them to babysit,

As I Am: Accepting Myself in an Unacceptable Society

I would bring up how I sure wish I had my blood relatives around cause I, missed them so much. I would talk about that and mention in between all the legit reasons I did miss them, how it would be cool to have them close to help with watching my son too, for times I wanted to make plans or whatever.

Well, the person would probably start feeling the sad feelings I had expressed about missing family and because they couldn't change that - they would offer to watch my kid, since that was something they could do. By that point they may have felt a little sorry for me. I had no idea I was playing a victim card. I did not see it as that because I was just expressing how I honestly missed my blood family that all live in other states. It wasn't like I was flat out saying my life was awful and I wanted people to feel sorry for me, at least I had never seen it as such. But truth was that I was still absolutely playing the victim - choosing my words carefully, hoping that I would say something to tug at the person's emotions leading to them offering to help! That's manipulation at its finest even though it doesn't seem like textbook manipulation. If the person didn't offer, then I'd let it be. It wasn't like I was carrying on, and because of that, to myself it wasn't manipulating. I wholeheartedly was not aware that this was a form of manipulation. It was just what I had learned that worked for me to get what I wanted; well one of many things I suppose. It's kind of funny when I look back at it because now it seems so silly to me. Annnnd NOW I would call this code talking, and all close to me know I DO NOT SPEAK IN CODE. If I say something out loud, I am not secretly hinting about that thing. I am saying it out loud so I can hear it and not forget! HA.

Can you even catch how subtle this technique can be? Now this was something I did in other ways too and it seriously took me years to realize what this was. So that whole "hinting around" hoping someone will catch your drift, yea - STOP IT! It is manipulation. It can be used in a funny way, if you are willing to immediately call it what it is. Same goes for actual guilt trips. Those can be so sly and subtle as well. They can also be totally innocent and playful IF you call them as they are and admit in the moment that that is exactly what you are doing. But to do them and only claim to be joking after someone else gets angry or calls you out? AFTER you deny the truth a few times - is not joking.

That's you not wanting to look like you were doing the behavior that is stigmatized. I am here to tell you - YOU ARE NOT ALONE. YOU CAN CHANGE THESE habits.

You just must be open and willing to admit and acknowledge them.

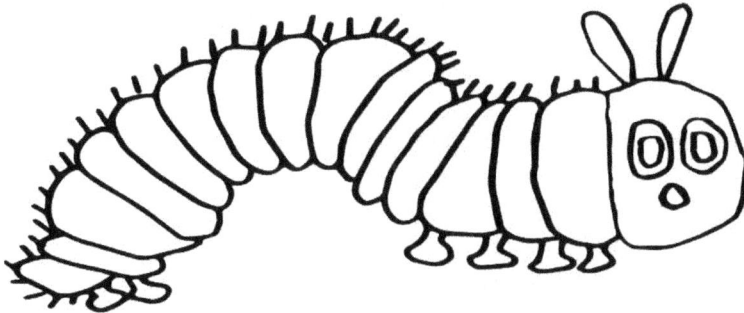

Now maybe your negative traits or defense tendencies are different than I mentioned, but hopefully you understand the point. I am going to provide you with some resources that truly blessed my life and allowed me to become so much more aware of these tendencies. Now, I am one of the most direct and blunt people you will ever meet. So much so, that some people do not like me because I am that direct. It is sometimes amusing because I will come straight out and ask you if you said something out of sarcasm or if I am annoying you, or whatever because I absolutely do not ever want to turn back to my old habits.

I am also very quick to call out other people when they attempt to use these tactics on me, or anything that remotely resembles them. Sometimes I do so too harshly, and we will get more into that during another section. I am not a perfect person and all people deserve grace no matter how difficult it is to extend that to them. Once we completely walk away from negative patterns, we are quick to forget how we were and tend to not have patience with others. I do my best to always remember where I was without allowing myself to slide back to that place. It has served me well when helping others, but even I must be reminded to show a little more mercy and grace to others at times. Occasionally, MORE REMINDED THAN I'D LIKE TO ADMIT! I AM HUMAN. I have bad days, and moments when I like to think some alien must've stolen my brain because I truly know better now. BUT that does not EQUAL perfection. It equals progression and being willing to do what's right when we KNOW we first did what was wrong.

As I Am: Accepting Myself in an Unacceptable Society

See we all have these negative traits or tendencies. What I have noticed along my road in life is that too many of us deny these things. We simply refuse to admit we behave the way we do. For various reasons we deny our own facets of our personalities, and honestly the only one we are fooling is ourselves. Other people see these things about us, they usually are not as quick to call things out because people don't want to be "rude" or feel it isn't their place. Well, that does us no justice I assure you, however, I do understand one thing- if a person is not ready to hear the truth and the WHOLE truth, they will flat not listen. I want to remind you; YOU are not that somebody if you are reading this. At least if you are, you are going to slowly learn to not be because you are reading this with an open and willing mind.

You are choosing to read this because you wanted to experience a greater level of self-acceptance and authentic, genuine self-love. You are going to listen and dig deep within yourself, asking your higher power or whatever means of faith you hold for guidance so that you can get the fullness this book has to offer you. Right?! Good!

Again, it's okay if you have different beliefs than mine, but this is my book, so you get my perspective. I believe that because we have one Creator, we all have Him within us. It is then part of our journey here to be active within Him. I believe that God in us is how people can access supernatural. I do believe Jesus is the bridge for mankind to be able to activate that within, but I also respect other beliefs. I am not typically traditional either, and I feel as a western society we discredit many eastern practices that are biblical as being not. I think that is just the enemy's way to keep Christians from fully experiencing God. I add this because I want all people to feel they can read this and take something away. I want you to know I believe that it is the God within us that gives us the ability to make the changes we need to, and I firmly believe I would not be where I am had I not had divine help from my higher power, my God.

So besides keeping you in the dark about your own actual behavior, let's look at what denial does to us. I want to start by asking you a question. Have you ever gotten super defensive when someone said something to you or asked you something? I mean defensive to the point you don't even know where your attitude came from, but you clearly saw that you got ugly with that person for no apparent reason. Hold that thought and let me ask you another question:

Has someone ever teased you about something you do and when they begin to tease you, suddenly you are spouting off this stuttering explanation of why you are justified in what they are teasing you about?

You don't think or feel that they are being very funny, and you MUST defend yourself. Those are two examples that you are in denial about something internally. I am providing some solid resources that go much deeper into the topic of denial because this is such a vital first step for us along our journey to authentically accepting and loving ourselves. As we are, where we are, how we are right now. It's like this, if you aren't willing to step out of denial even if you realize you might not be that person Denial is an authentic blocker!

Let me also remind you of this truth; to admit these things about yourself does NOT mean these traits or behaviors now define you. I think that's why so many of us hold on to that denial so strongly. I can remember thinking there was no way I was manipulating people and playing the victim card. I was not a manipulative person; I was not some, *"Feel sorry for me" type girl! I couldn't be! I did a lot of great and sacrificial things for others!"* Truth is, I was. Truth is, I did a lot of great things for people with the wrong motive... Truth is, yes, I made sacrifices and did so often, but I had an alternative motive without ever even realizing it. Even though I did not like this truth, there was a TRUTH that outweighed that- I still was a good, decent person! I was simply HUMAN. HA! Imagine that! We often categorize or even label ourselves based on these negative traits and behaviors because that is what society does! We clump ourselves into these little boxed communities of labels and we will build our identity from these labels. We need to recognize AND STOP doing that; but let's face it, that is a difficult task when everything around us in society is cultivating that ideology. Labels, tags, diagnoses, disorders, more labels. Everyone talks about how they are labeled. I even brought up the way I think being ADD/ADHD is more of a way of how my brain works and sometimes a superpower. For many it's another label. Another "REASON" to not take FULL ownership of their own actions and personal responsibility to work on themselves becoming a better SELF. Can I be a little REAL TALK with y'all right now? Good, 'cause I am going to anyway. LOOK DEEP into all the REASONS you personally give for why you are not able to do something... Take your time, this is an exercise strictly for you... ...

...

...

I SAY THIS WITH LOVE, AND OUT OF MY OWN PERSONAL WALK- THOSE ARE MOST ALL EXCUSES NOT ACTUAL VALID LEGIT REASONS.... Sure life happens, and we struggle. We have difficult situations to handle and many of us do not have adequate coping skills to handle a lot that we need to. HOWEVER, we live in a time information is accessible literally at the click of our pretty fingers. We live in a time we should not have SO MANY REASONS for not doing things that will help us. ESPECIALLY WHEN we KNOW we need help! I'M JUST SAYING!!!!!!!!!!!!

Listen, you do not have to allow these undesirable tendencies to be WHO YOU ARE. You only must admit them and see them as they are so that you can fully accept yourself, YOUR WHOLE SELF, AS YOU ARE. AS I AM.

As I Am: Accepting Myself in an Unacceptable Society

For these reasons and so many more we need to be aware of what we feed our souls. Soul, as I know it, means our mind, will, and emotions collectively. What are we listening to, watching, and thinking about? What kind of people do we hang around? What does the music we listen to say? I know I am going to be a little old school here and remind you that it all matters! Every word spoken you hear or read influences you. No matter how great the beat in a song is, what are the lyrics saying? IT ALL goes into our subconscious whether we believe it. It all takes a part in shaping what we think and how we feel even if we want to deny that too. I am not telling you that you cannot or should not listen to your favorite gangsta rap song or watch your drama show. I am saying take inventory of it all, and balance it out with MORE POSITIVE messages, ADD some uplifting stuff in there if need be. THAT IS ALL.

Watch less news, eat more veggies so to speak. We feed our soul just like we feed our physical self. WHAT ARE YOU FEEDING YOUR SOUL??

It's amazing how once we step out of this thing known as denial, suddenly we can receive information in a way that helps us reprogram our thinking. It's then that those behaviors begin fading away right before our very eyes. It's somewhat magical how that happens, and usually people don't believe it until they live it out. Even then we still are skeptical, because there is this constant nagging force yapping in our head or whispering garbage in our ear. That's what I call the enemy of humanity, the negative force many call Satan or the devil. See he whispers to us all, no matter race or color or faith belief. He whispers because he knows if you ever shut out his negative nagging, and you get a hold of WHO you really are by listening to our Creator's voice within you, he is defeated! Sadly, I found that he doesn't even have to whisper much. Most of the time I fabricated the crap all by myself. I think the enemy will twist one small thing, and then what happens is we ourselves run wild with that twist, with that poison.

Negative thinking is literally poison to our bodies, as negative thoughts release negative hormones. This is SCIENCE FOLKS, not hypothetical. In Dr. Caroline Leaf's book, "How to Switch On Your Brain," she gives such great explanations of how our thinking affects us. I really recommend reading her book or looking up her research on YouTube. AGAIN, even if you differ in faith, the woman talks a lot of brain science and SHE

69

KNEWS HER STUFF. I gained so much insight and understanding from this book. It is just really mind blowing to me how we tend to create our own doom and gloom. In a society looking to pass the buck, and place blame, it's easier for us to blame the enemy than take ownership. I am here to tell you, the enemy may plant a negative seed, but we are the ones responsible for what we do with it. Generally, we feed it, nurture it and then we are these grouchy bitter people. Sometimes worse we live in torment of depression, anxiety, and countless other mental anguishes all because we feed those negative seeds that WE DO NOT HAVE TO, FOLKS. We have a choice!

B

O

D   M

Y   O   U   R

V

E

INTERACTION TIME

MOVE YOUR BODY someway physically! Set the book down, stretch, do some intentional deep breathing. Maybe grab some peppermints to enjoy during the next section's reading, or yummy sugar free candy. Also light a candle, or turn on your essential oil diffuser, or whatever method of room smelly goods you use, this way as you continue you are also activating your sense of smell and taste.

As I Am: Accepting Myself in an Unacceptable Society

Denial keeps emotions trapped. Mental illness is defined as chemical imbalances in short, would you agree? Well, emotions release various chemicals in our bodies. I noted some great books and websites to look up regarding this.

Denial gives you a twisted view of others and the world around you. (remember those rose-colored glasses I mentioned earlier) You remember those questions about getting defensive? Think back to those.

Can you honestly look at your answer and say that you don't perceive others to be this way since you are? Think on that...

...   .

Yes. I mean really think on that! Don't skip to the next page...

but THINK...

We do. That's another thing we tend to forget, how we view ourselves REALLY, is how we view the world and those around us. Don't believe me, just take some time to observe after reading this far. Look up some of the information on denial and read it. Then take several days to observe your own tendencies and thought patterns. Now you might say this doesn't affect your physical well-being, but it does! What happens when we are judging people or our world negatively? What happens when we see others through a twisted lens based on our own behaviors and shortcomings? We wrongly perceive them, right? We judge them before we fully know them. We even shun them for sometimes no valid reasons at all, simply because we see them as we see ourselves. Don't believe me just look at all the failed marriages; I speak from experience. Sure they fail for many reasons, but I would put money on it that most failed marriages are because of wrongfully interpreting one another, not understanding each other most might say. One projects their insecurities onto the other, and it becomes a vicious cycle.

You see, you can live in denial, but deep down you know you are denying something so then you feel like you're a fake. It's a whole cascade of garbage that is rooted in mostly lies. There is a Christian 12-step program called Celebrate Recovery that has an abundance of great tools and resources especially related to topic of denial. I have included some resources to that program. Yes, it's a 12-step recovery program, but honestly, it's for so much more than only addictions and substance abuse problems. In the material it gives acronyms for a lot of words, and the one for denial is a personal favorite. This is out of their step study book, and it's also in their Celebrate Recovery bible. My favorite tool through them has been their Celebrate Recovery Daily Devotional, and I have read tons of various devotionals over the years. This one is still top in my life.

Denial keeps us isolated and alienated from others. Especially from the people closest to us. There are so many things denial steals from us. It not only adds to our drama and pain, but it makes it hurt longer. It keeps us bound to chains of anxiety and unwarranted stress far longer than if we just deal with the thing we are denying. Denial doesn't actually protect us from painful emotions or feelings, it turns them numb. What comes to mind is when you sit on your foot for a long time and it goes numb. You know that pins and needle feeling it gets? Yea it doesn't really hurt, but it doesn't feel good either, right? This is sort of what denial does to our emotions when we are in denial. There is this whole part of the brain called the limbic system and information I have read regarding that explain very well how emotions affect us. It is very interesting and made me analyze so much the more I learned about it. All this denying leads to us feeling a sense of fatigue, and we get totally energy drained! Which of course just leads to more negative crap. It really is just one cycle of negative mess after another. I don't know about you guys, but I really cannot afford to lose any more energy in life. Denial does that too, it drains us of our energy. Put these things together and it stunts growth. Period. You cannot move forward to flourish and deal with new life circumstances or situations if you are numb, and fatigued. You can't process natural life events normal to experience in healthy or stable ways if you are stuck in another emotional level of life. Denial flat keeps us STUCK, and I believe with my whole heart it's doing more damage to more of us than we think.... So think about that.

As I Am: Accepting Myself in an Unacceptable Society

Let's use the example I mentioned earlier. That I was in denial about talking excessively. Now people that are close to me know I have this tendency, and most of them just overlook it. Occasionally someone would mention it to me, but I would go into defensive mode and shut them down. Because remember I am in denial about this. Well, because I am trying to hide from the believing I talk too much, I tend to just not talk to people at all. I begin to isolate myself. I might go around them still, but I just really keep my mouth shut and comment very little. I only speak when I am directly asked something, or if I need to ask for something or whatever. SO I can still be around people, but I am isolating myself still because I am afraid if I say too much at any time someone will confirm what I am trying to deny. Another thing is in this, I am denying myself to share my voice with close friends. And honestly what is a relationship without people exchanging their views and perspective? This is something I believe society has forgotten with all our social media. We forget that to build real, long lasting relationships of any form we must experience the exchange of ideas, opinions, PERSPECTIVE. I digress.

As I Am: Accepting Myself in an Unacceptable Society

Worn out yet? I am. Lol.

Denial is a nasty thing. It leads to false beliefs, false images of ourselves and others, and basically a false life! It is serious too, and I often see many people think a little denial never hurts, but I don't agree. I hate admitting to myself and others certain things, but since I learned how to, it's absolutely freeing. It is important to note that I don't admit these truths to everyone I meet either. I admit them to myself first and to God. At the end of every day that's most important to me! I then do find my person, my confidant. Occasionally other people are okay to admit certain things to also, but the list of who you admit what to should be limited. The point is not to go around wearing it anymore, to admit it and acknowledge it in order to free yourself from its unspoken power.

As I Am: Accepting Myself in an Unacceptable Society

Finding My Way…

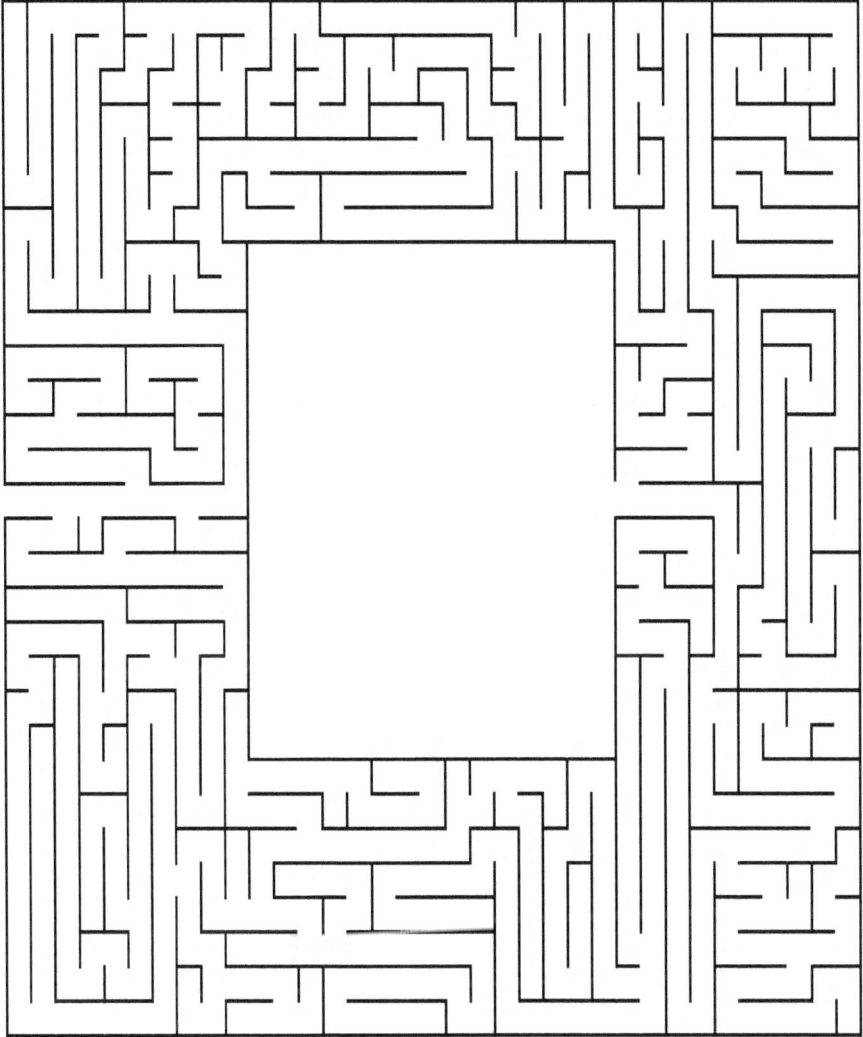

Social Media Myths

"Everyone needs a tribe. But how do you attract the attention of others?"

(Jeff Goins)

It seems odd to me that we all know social media is intended for entertainment, as well as a way to connect to others far away, but it is still taken so seriously. I mean the statistics of people who end up in serious depression and self-harm because of said social media bullies is insanely high. I will admit that I too get sucked into scrolling aimlessly through Facebook or Instagram without realizing how much time I have spent or more importantly how much it has affected my psyche. Many times I will go stalk childhood friends' pages and see what their lives are up to out of curiosity. I will look up people I once was close to but lost contact with for whatever reason to attempt reconnecting. No harm, no foul right? Well, sure if I could honestly tell you that there weren't times as I scrolled through people's posts and pictures and felt jealous, sad, disappointed, angry, envious, or any other number of negative feelings. I was never one who thought I looked through social media and believed only the image people wanted the world to see, but somehow it seeped into my subconscious without my actual intention.

I would go through the posts of those childhood friends or classmates and think about the mistakes or paths I choose in my younger years. I would think about how I should have been closer to this person or stayed away from another person. I did not ever see this as harmful because in the moment it was innocent, or so I thought. In the moment, I found myself reflecting on what my life was, is, and could have been based on the lives I saw my peers living on their social media. Remember, comparison is a thief! I never thought of it as detrimental, but oh how it created me to be unhappy and dissatisfied with my present life! It added to the "idea" of my life being a failure since I was not in the same places that my classmates were. It reminded me how my choices as a teen landed me into being a single mom.

I don't remember feeling jealous or envious until random moments when I wasn't even scrolling. It would be moments when life randomly hit me and my lack of coping with things in a healthy way kicked in. At those times, my mind would replay all those schoolmates who I saw having these amazing life experiences, with love, support and self-efficiency. My mind would even replay the ones I came across who I wrongly judged. I would think, "Surely I deserved better than them! They were jerks in school." Then I would self-hate because of feelings of inadequacy, as if I was nothing but a complete failure. I would lose all memory of the things I did have in my life, although they weren't documented - 'cause, well I was too busy enjoying life. But it was like all I could think about was what my life was not. I mean, this is not at all a way to live, and especially not a way to thrive in this life.

When I think back, I did the very thing I despised others for doing. I would scroll through this platform that was intended to share happy, joyful memories with friends and family, and I would judge! Here was another area I believed lies about myself. Just like I never thought I was a negative person, only to find out that in reality I spoke HORRIBLY in regard to myself. I also thought I was not judgmental; and, well, maybe I wasn't judgmental in the open sense such as when you see someone and categorize them first by appearance. I did not judge someone when they would share with me the difficult secrets they kept hidden from the world because they were ashamed. I did not judge people by their past mistakes or currently poor choices. Nevertheless, how I judged was my own secret and it kept me from the internal freedom I always THOUGHT I had. I would scroll and judge people based on my own understanding of their lives and circumstances. I would stalk their joyful pictures thinking about how I KNEW they did not SOW the kind of seeds I SOWED in life, so how did they reap these beautiful blessings I continued to fall short of. SAD, right? Mean, even! Who the heck was I to be thinking I KNEW anything at all about what these people sowed in their lives?! But I feel like I am not alone in this…… (*crickets, as you get real with YOURSELF*)

I judged them based on my own EXTREMELY limited knowledge of their lives, and I felt justified in doing so! I was continually eating the very poison I called out in others. I was using social media as a measuring stick in a manner of speaking, and I was only doing more damage to my inner self without EVEN realizing it. Remember - I am that person who, for years, talked to others about not doing this very thing. I was the one who knew WHO I was and as far as I was concerned, I had this healthy handle on my life. HA! It was so clear how untrue that idea was!!! BUT you see- I did not see it then. Isn't this one of those moments the old saying comes into play, "Hindsight is 20/20"? However, I would like to encourage you not to get stuck in your hindsight. If we aren't careful, we can get stuck there and then misjudged the progress that we have made by looking at what we perceive as errors; creating another unhealthy cycle. It may look different, but it will be the same.

The truth is, social media has an actual purpose. It can serve us, but we must be disciplined and see it for what it is. We must be willing to acknowledge that it can very easily become an addiction and gets out of balance without us noticing. Social media was designed for various reasons, and I am not here to tell you what those reasons are specifically. I am here to remind you to take social media at face value and with a grain of salt. I am here to remind you that you can be intentional about not overusing it, you can be intentional about not allowing yourself to get trapped in the "their life is better than mine" or whatever judgment you tend to make. I am here to tell you that it does not have to be a measuring stick for what is "normal" in YOUR life. You just must start with facing the truth about it for yourself. You have to start with recognizing the areas that are out of alignment, recognizing your own thoughts that pass through your mind as you scroll on the social forum of your choice; and you must also take into account the thoughts that will randomly run through our minds because of social media WHEN WE ARE NOT ACTUALLY SCROLLING! (Everything we take in through our eyes and ears affects us, EVERYTHING.)

We tend to believe very one sided these days, and truth is no matter how the world looks, no matter the number listed in the statistics, nothing is ever one sided or one specific way. I read a short article, "5 Myths About Young People and Technology", which I am inserting the link with hope you will read it as well:

[https://www.psychologytoday.com/us/blog/freedom-learn/201402/five-myths-about-young- people-and-social-media]

This article hit home hard for me, not because I have a son who is now over 18, but because it opened my eyes to view this very topic in a way I often failed to see it. I am guilty of this too, but we as parents and older generations have this tendency to blame technology for our kids lack social interactions, yet we are the ones keeping them sheltered. I see it in so many families I personally know. I am aware I struggled with this too, but I will say that I made more effort than not to send my son outside on his bike, and to mingle when his friends were able. He went through being bullied even, and I made him learn how to respectfully stand up for himself. I encouraged dropping him and friends off at the mall, or movies and then calling for a ride when they were finished. Thankfully he does drive now because when he was younger there were no pay phones around like when I was growing up. And honestly many of the younger kids DO have cell phones, but there are plenty who don't! It's almost a catch 22 these days though. My son had a phone since he was 10 because we did not have a landline and he stayed home after school sometimes, so he needed a way to call me. What about the parents not wanting to give their 12-year old's cell phones though? Yes, there are plenty out there. My suggestion is to utilize the parent controls! Get phones that cannot use the internet or block certain things, limit texting, etc. Thing is there are still ways to keep your kids safe with cell phones ALONG with keeping your bill down! You just must ASK the right questions to the phone service people. Again, another soap box for a different day! HA.

In this following section I talk about how social media is taken out of context and has, to some degree, cost us our interpersonal skills. When I read the article I cited above, I am reminded that the biggest myth of all social media and the news media, is that this world is so much worse off than it is. From that article I was given a new perspective of our teens and young adults in regards to technology and social media, and it reminded me that we are living in the biggest state of fear we've seen in decades - maybe even ever, and the truth is our kids are probably the safest in history. Yet we have socially isolated them and blamed the technology we hand them to keep them content while we "adult.". I am aware that the study discussed in the article is not the entire teen population, but the facts about crime rates are by no means fake. We have created a society where fear is the driving force, and we cannot see it for what it is. We have all this access to information, yet we cannot see the world is in many ways better than it once was.

As I Am: Accepting Myself in an Unacceptable Society

REMEMBER now we hear about much more because of the access to information at our fingertips. Yes, we have had more school shootings, and teenage suicides, but what we don't hear about is kids being kidnapped from malls, or young women coming up missing from grocery stores because of serial killers wanting to cut and wear their skin! Do any of us stop and think about the environment we have created around our children for them to be so engaged in their phones and tablets. It isn't all the world's fault, and it certainly isn't all the technology's either.

Please do not get me wrong, I am very aware of all the insane stories of violence out there. The thing is much of it can be prevented! WE NEED TO TAKE SOME STUFF a little more serious though. We must stop burying our heads in the sand pretending things will just get better or go away. Just the same we cannot go around picketing and screaming about congress creating new laws. New laws are NOT THE ANSWER necessarily. Hear me out before you roll your eyes at me. First, we need to GET OFF OUR PHONES WHILE WE DRIVE!! ALL OF US! I see just as many adults on theirs as younger people, so this isn't a blame game

As I Am: Accepting Myself in an Unacceptable Society

OKAY! WE need to ACT accordingly like serious! When I investigate stories of violence and scary shit like shootings, you know what I find?? People who are broken and hurting. Granted, I am NOT excusing their actions either, BUT I am telling you this- THERE ARE ALWAYS warning signs! There is more WE AS INDIVIDUALS CAN DO! SHOULD DO! NO, you cannot force people to get help, however, when we are kind, loving, and inclusive towards others we can make a difference in their lives... Individually we have a voice, yet so often we fall into the belief, "my voice does not matter so I will just accept this and move on." GUESS WHAT I CALL BS. If someone treats you unjustly you can make a formal complaint without being EXTRA. There is just a way to do things. You just must find the RIGHT person to talk to.

There is a lot of crap I know we cannot change, but the one thing I know we can do is utilize OUR PERSONAL responsibility as UNITED STATES CITIZENS for how we ACT, THINK, AND BEHAVE!!!!!!!! Stop worrying about petty things and LOOK AT WHAT MATTERS! The emotional intelligence in this country has drastically decreased, and I cannot even apologize folks, but at the end of the day - THAT IS probably one of the biggest problems with our country! AND WE HAVE TO STOP BLAMING, and simply act towards ownership and personal responsibility!

This is another example of how we are unintentionally cultivating an environment of our own fears for our children, because we do not realize how much garbage we are taking in through our own social media (or media exposure in general). We have fabricated the most unforeseen scenarios based on all the CSI programs we watch faithfully, scary movies we take in on a regular basis for FUN, the news we feel we must watch in order to stay in the "KNOW" with our world's events, etc. We have not taken 5 minutes to properly weed or sort through any of the junk we so aimlessly consume, and it has affected the way we treat and raise our children all while we sit back and blame everything else. It isn't about blame though; I need to make that clear. It isn't our fault or technology's fault. It isn't even our teens' faults. It is our responsibility that has slipped by us. We have a responsibility to our children, and what we have done is allowed our own fears from false realities and over blown information to cloud our view. We have allowed ourselves to believe everything we see or hear and worked so hard to protect our children from the world. Then we sit here and wonder why they can't adult and why remain immature!

We ARE MISSING IT PEOPLE! It is the world WE created for them because WE don't know how to take in social media, or news media. WE have lost ourselves in the midst of all the technology, and we simply need to take some time to breath and check ourselves! It starts with us! We need to learn balance folks. We need to stop believing that the world is going to engulf our children, or that dirt causes infections! LAST TIME I CHECKED, DIRT DON'T HURT! Do you realize how many studies have shown that because parents have gotten so obsessed and overboard with diseases and germs, now our children are sicker than ever because they never were able to build their immune system! WE HAVE TO WAKE UP! EVEN MORE - how many of the very products we are using to clean and protect our children and families ARE ACTUALLY THE SOURCE of harm; more than what we THINK we are protecting from? The evidence is INSANELY strong people, and what have we done? We have buried our heads. It's amusing to me how so many of the people I know and meet complain about the system of government we have but turn right around and fully trust everything stated by them without FIRST even researching for themselves! I mean, if YOU THINK the powers that be are liars, and do not really care for us as people WHY IN THE HECK do you trust the products (or whatever) out there these same people tell you are "SAFE" for you?????????????

You know, many holler at political rallies, "Make America Great AGAIN!" but can I tell you something? One president cannot change a country of millions of people. One political party cannot make America a better place to live over the other political party. What CAN make America great again is each and every one of us taking our responsibilities as Americans back; being willing to face each other even if we don't want to. Better yet, being willing to admit that we also spend too much time watching TV, playing phone games, or scrolling social media. We need to stop lying to ourselves folks! If you are sitting there saying, "Well, I watch the news on TV and like maybe 2 shows, that's a pretty good balance considering what's out there" - you are right, that's not a bad balance, but what are you doing with what you watch? Do you watch the news and those shows, and then put something positive in front of yourself to counter that? Do you watch the news, and then actually research what you saw to find out the actual or semi factual parts that the news so conveniently leaves out because they want us only to know the part that keeps us stuck in fear! Do you internalize what you have looked at, allowing all these envious thoughts fill your head? What are you doing to bring balance to the lies that are set before you or the false facts that keep you up at night? How are you coping with the child trafficking post you just had to read that came across Facebook? How many times have you seen that post that says a celebrity died only to find out it was fake?! HELLO?!!! Does that not show you that the media will find a way to put false information before you to keep you in fear even if it's so subtle that you will only think it's harmless? Better yet, we call it ENTERTAINMENT! (Insert the emoji slapping its face.) AND LET ME NOT EVEN GET ON TOPIC OF ADVERTISEMENT!

Color Me Calm...

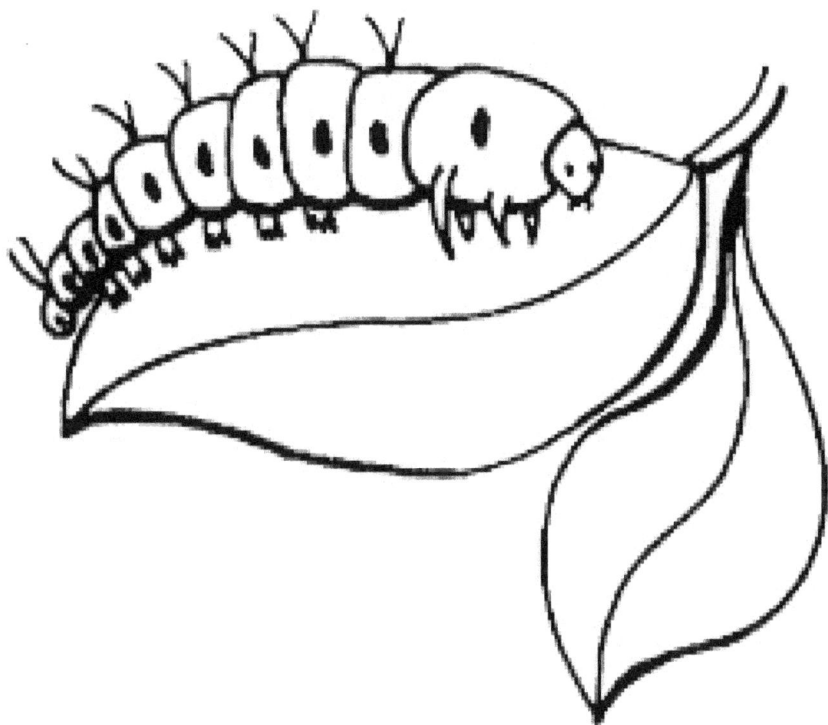

As I Am: Accepting Myself in an Unacceptable Society

We have become like my little caterpillar friends. We are simply going around consuming all the junk around us, while never ACTUALLY researching to confirm TRUTH or confront LIES. Most of all - we are never confronting what is TWISTED to suit someone else's agenda! We are just chomping away at all the 'leaves', talking foolishly and mindlessly at times; because we THINK it's satisfying our current event knowledge, but it only has us believing lies! It starts with us! It starts with getting ourselves back to the basics in life, and reevaluating WHO we are really. It begins with us not being gullible to believe everything someone says just because of who says it.

Social media isn't bad, and it isn't causing us to lose connection with each other, we are causing that. We are choosing to live in a world that isolates us to our little circle in order to keep ourselves and families "safe"; yet are we really safe? I mean if we can't process emotional confrontation, and we can't maturely debate or discuss differences in opinions or views, then to me our psyche is just as unsafe as if we were standing next to a crazed, physically abusive person. We are losing our mental health, and our children are the ones suffering the most because we are not properly loving ourselves! Our children learn from watching us more than listening to us. They learn what is acceptable, and tolerable by what we accept and tolerate. Yes, I KNOW this is a pretty scary thought, right? A lot of this happens at a subconscious level, which is why many of us don't actually notice it. That is, until we are forced to do the whole hindsight 20/20 mess. Pretty sure there should be a BEFORE HINDSIGHT to AVOID hindsight thing, whatta think? If you can't see the connection, then maybe this book isn't for you. Because at the end of the day, finding myself and truly loving and accepting myself has been the one single thing that has made me a better mom. It is where our "freedom" comes from, and I don't take lightly what our Veterans have sacrificed or done for us, but I believe when we allow ourselves to get so lost in the false expectations shoved in our face through "entertainment" and technology, then we are willingly giving up those freedoms the Veterans so selflessly fight to protect. Personal freedom leads to inner peace. When I AUTHENTICALLY FELT this deep self-acceptance, I broke free from comparisons, and doubt. I was able to shake lose the thoughts that often attacked me causing so much self-sabotage which meant I was coping with life in healthier ways. I was finding it easier to make wise decisions. When we are living in our personal FREEDOM, we worry less. We become more loving, gracious, and more forgiving towards those around us. We become better examples for our children.

One of the weirdest things to me we ALL experiences is when I see, hear, or sometimes even THINK about someone yawning and BAM! I yawn... (AHH – LIKE I literally just did while typing this out! Ha). FOLKS, there is research about this and to me it explains a ton of various things I experience and observe. It also proves to some degree why everything we see has the impact it does on us. Interesting enough we do have mirror neuron receptors in our brains. When I learned about this, I thought soooooooo why ain't I using this MORE in everyday life? Did a little more research, of course, and found a YouTube video by Mel Robbins. She was speaking about how to make yourself do what you do not want to do. She told her audience to do a test for themselves that involved them picking 2 people a day to make eye contact with and give the person the biggest genuine smile.

As I Am: Accepting Myself in an Unacceptable Society

So I did this myself over the following week. I did not WANT to look these complete strangers in the eyes and give them some CHEESY grin. I am a people person, but after working as a phlebotomist for so many years, I learned NOT to look strangers in the eyes. PS a phlebotomist is the person who draws your blood when the doctor orders labs. In the setting I worked in, people did 1 of 2 things. Either they had to look the opposite direction while I drew their blood, leaving me to talk to them while barely seeing their face at all, OR they would take my eye contact as an unspoken invitation to share the LONGEST story about WHO KNOWS WHAT while I had a waiting room FULL of HANGRY people ready to GO. I did it though. I committed to myself that I would give this mirror neuron exercise a try, in the attempt to also practice JUST DOING something I didn't want to do. The results...

The results are worth you seeing for yourself! Now I am challenging you to give it a shot!

SO let me ask you then, why don't we use this more often for the greater good? I feel like we should do this, and then also test it with a frown, although that may be more obviously noted than what renders a test. I can tell you without any doubt, I feel like when someone is grouchy everyone grouchy seems to come out that day. She also talks about how we make decisions within 5 seconds, so count back from 5 then do what it is you need to. She is the author of 'The 5 Second Rule", which is a great read.

So maybe the test is to take those people and go beyond a big smile. Maybe we get around those people and find someone overly negative to encourage them to turn their frown upside down. Maybe in the social media world, this means we can share our joyful happy moments, but at the same time we can share some of our not so happy moments as well to let others know, "Hey, we are real and sometimes life is not all puppies and rainbows." It's all about balance; something that seems out of reach in today's society. It also seems that when we read or learn about new things that it's good for us to test that out when possible. In this case it's not terribly difficult to smile intentionally at new people, in order to see how many will indeed return the smile. SO what do we have to lose doing it, a little of our "pride"? For me, it helps me gain a deeper understanding of how important my attitude and my demeanor are in the world I exist in. I can't be the only one who will feel better knowing that I made an impact in another person's life simply by locking eye contact with them and smiling from ear to ear; genuinely, from deep within me, expecting nothing in return. The motive is to simply impact someone else for the better. (To see the mirror test in effect, but you must be genuinely wanting to brighten someone else's life at the heart of this and to take some steps in doing things with intention EVEN WHEN you don't WANT or FEEL like it.)

As I sit and think about this exercise, I go back to speaking more positively about myself and about the power in our speech overall. When you read the studies on these mirror neurons in our brains, you see the smile works. We all know about yawning after we see or even hear another do it, and we know that energy itself is contagious. SO why would speech not do the same thing? For instance I mentioned realizing one day how negatively I spoke about myself, and what was interesting was that once I saw this about myself, it became more obvious that the people around me also spoke of themselves more this way as well! Keep in mind though, we cannot fix anyone else! It is not our job to judge or try and change anyone else, only ourselves. Alright, but you will notice habits in others that you can relate to once you begin working to change those habits within yourself; so what do you do with that? What if I told you, *"You do nothing!"* Here is the thing, the mirror neurons are going to be activated in others when you are around them right?

[https://www.psychologytoday.com/us/blog/the-couch/201303/empathy-understanding-and- mirror-neurons]

Right, so you continue to focus on your own speech, your own way of seeing life and yourself, and as you grow you will influence those around you naturally. I am seeing this happen every day it's really amazing. Those that want to grow and expand their lives will notice the positive changes in you and will begin making changes in their lives also. There will be those that are just so full of toxins and negativity that they will be the ones most likely to drift apart from your life altogether. This can be sad, and disappointing, but it's inevitable. The absolute best thing for us to do is pray life and blessings over these people. Forgive them, speak for health and joy to follow them, so that one day they will be able to step into a world that is full of light, peace, joy, and most of all true love. I am not saying you don't share this new discovery with your close friends or keep your new journey on the down low. I am just saying that we cannot go around trying to help people wake up just because we see something in them, we used to struggle with. This has been something that caused me to push several great people completely out of my life, and I had to realize that it is a journey each of us must do in our own timing. No matter how miserable someone is, and how much I think I can offer them a way out of that misery, unless they are ready to leave it and they reach out willingly, then I am only to love them and pray for them; as they are, wherever they are! Even when they reach out, for me I must be careful not to go right into counsel or lecture mode. Here's the thing, God is love and His love is truly unconditional, therefore when the Bible tells us to love others as God loves us, we are to love them without conditions. That also means we are not to condemn or lecture them. Sure there is a time for correction, but I am learning that mostly isn't my job either. The way I show love best is when I treat others how I believe God's love has first treated me. This isn't easy when we don't fully grasp it, or we have been taught something contrary. Even the most well-meaning people get this concept wrong too often, and that is why we have a world full of those who do not truly understand loving themselves fully, let alone loving others.

INTERACT WITH ME!

Take out the journal or use these lines to write down 3 things you have heard on the news or some form of information you listen to or watch that you can research for yourself instead of taking what the media says as truth. Jot the date down that you are at this point and give yourself a week out to find credible sources outside what you typically listen or read. Need help? Check out my website for more resources.

As I Am: Accepting Myself in an Unacceptable Society

So the more we understand about these mirror neurons we all have, the more it makes sense that we will attract what (who) we are. When you understand these little mirror neurons you understand why it's said we are the sum of the 5 closest people we hang around most. When we understand these mirror neurons, we can understand why often times we are unable to pull people up to the positive level we are at. We may not have enough positive influences around us to start with. That means the 1 or 2 that need the most pulling up will end up pulling us down. In the psychology article I referenced a few paragraphs above, it said something I think is often forgotten these days: The therapist told his patient that he wanted to know what her feelings felt like for her because while he could empathize with the general feeling of sadness, he did not know what that felt like for another person. He explained his reasoning clearly and told the patient it also served a purpose to help her deal with her feelings more by having her articulate them. It's a short read but worth it.

Here's the point to this; whether you think this is all true or it's some scientific mambo jumbo, it's a thing, nonetheless. I am certain everyone acknowledges the yawn effect, and if you intentionally try the smile test then you will see that work as well. The bottom line is what are you allowing your eyes to look at? Social Media does not have to be a negative thing for any of us, just like any other form of entertainment, but what we need to do is wake up and realize is the fact that it affects us. It all makes some sort of impression in our brains even if it's the smallest of one. Those impressions can combine with other memories or impressions in our mind, and then create false thoughts of understanding or false realities for us. These false realities can combine and make us believe all sorts of things that aren't factual. They can combine without us knowing because they are being processed through the same filter. And the whole purpose is making you more aware of how you can finally sort through all the junk keeping you from fully accepting your own self.

BRAIN BREAK

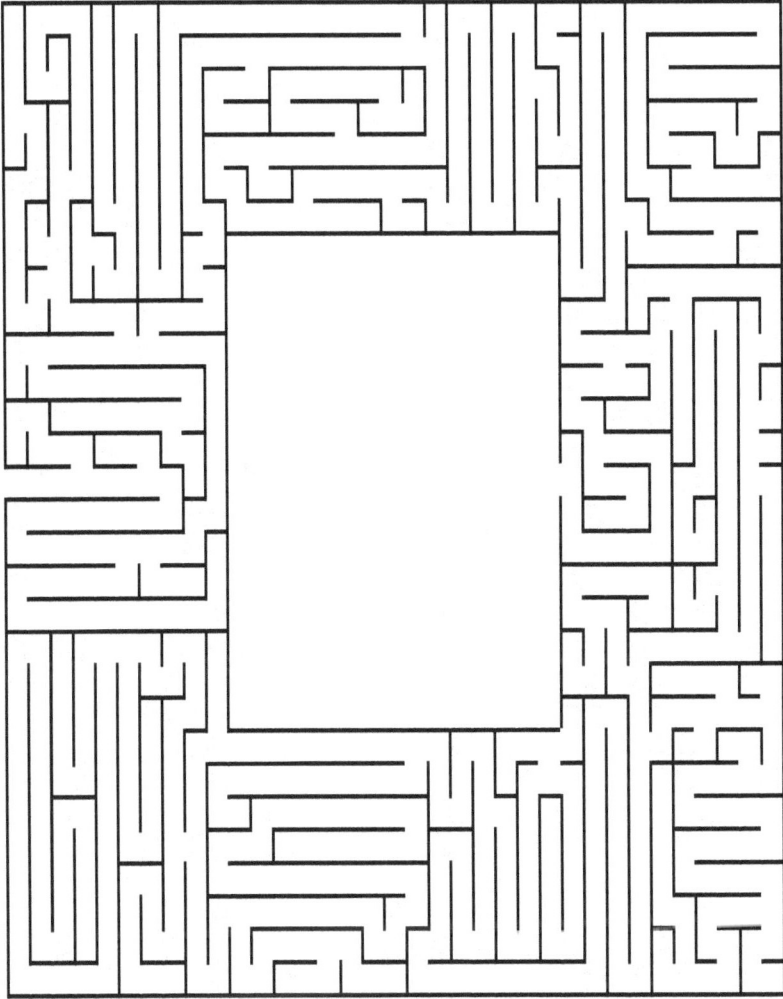

As I Am: Accepting Myself in an Unacceptable Society

So as I write about this, I want to ask a question regarding the long-debated topic of if violent video games or scary movies actually have a negative effect on us? Well, I am going to venture out to say they do, but like all things, balance will again be key. There is some truth to the whole desensitizing that happens when we allow too much non positive information and images enter our ear and eye gates. Have you ever been doing something and then this wild, insanely crazy idea pop through your head? For example, a thought like, "What would happen if I just randomly swerve my car into oncoming traffic on the other side of the highway?" I am being silly because most of us would say we would hit the other cars and it would cause a huge wreck. Alright, but did you ever think the things you watch on TV or seen scrolling through social media affected you in a similar way? What about having unrealistic fears about your children? How about that fear sneaking In, that technically is borderline paranoia, that something is going to happen to you each time you walk to your car in a dark parking lot late at night?

I hope you see where I am going with this. It's not that I am saying we need to give up our scary movie love or stop scrolling through social media or even watching the news. I am saying that everything matters that you expose yourself to. It all counts, and I just want you to see that because of how important it is to become more mindful of what you listen to, what you watch and look at, and what you allow yourself to believe. Do not quickly believe everything that you read or watch on the news channels. Do not quickly buy into someone's opinion simply because they are your spiritual leader or someone you greatly look up to. Do not allow yourself to spend more time in an entertainment world than in the real face to face world with loved ones. Be aware that some of the reasons we no longer like being around other people is because so many people do not accept and fully love themselves, therefore they continually vomit their baggage and insecurities over anyone around them. In order to shift that today we must start with ourselves, and then be the example; we must be the mirror others need to follow.

I would like to address another side of this social media myth busting, those who do not engage in it often. Or at least those who believe this. Please let me again say, I understand there are plenty of those people who truly do not get into social media at all or at least very little. My hat goes off to you and I suggest still reading this section because you may gain insight to help someone you know, or maybe you will just gain a tad more understanding for those who do post excessively in your view. Either way I will do my best to speak in a way that is relatable to everyone. I have also found that along my journey there are many out there who do not post excessively, but they scroll and stalk continually. So don't try to fool yourselves, BE HONEST!

I will be honest; I scroll Facebook way too much. I also post more than many like. It comes in waves for me, but if you ask certain people about it my goodness they would tell you it must be why I can't get anything else in my life accomplished because I live on social media, and well that is obviously not true. How did I make time to write this book? Or work on the craft projects I do? Or what about going back to school, or spending time with my son? I mean yes, I am fortunate enough to have a job that I get some days with a ton of down time, but that isn't every day. Plus, for me, I have found that it's a way for my family to keep in touch with me. I get mad about this at times because it causes my family to call less since they can keep up with me via social media, but it's helpful to a degree, nonetheless. However, I am not getting on social media as a junkie, stirring up arguments (although occasionally I will chime in on a thread that I later regret). I will also post stuff I would like to discuss with others, and that too usually turns into people taking me wrong and getting mad with me. But hey, generally I post uplifting, random, and family stuff.

For those of you reading this and genuinely do not struggle with any of the things I mentioned, I applaud you again. I would like to ask you to stay aware, that's all. Be careful of how you think about the ones you see filling up the feed with meme after meme or post after post. There are people out there who need this outlet. They need to express themselves through this medium because that's either all they know, or they just got sucked into the habit of doing it. We do best for others when we move from a place of questioning "why" they do the things they do, to a place of asking what I can do to make sure that person knows I care. You don't have to care about their junk or baggage either. I am not telling you to pick up their issues and enable them. I am simply asking you to get away from a standpoint of judgment (which is what we are doing when we ask why people do whatever it is, we see is inappropriate) and instead simply send that person a message or post saying, "Hello! Thinking of you!"

If social media isn't a problem for you, be thankful!

Some people have no close relatives by them, others are not as social in public life, so they are more comfortable behind the safety of the virtual world. Does it bother me that we have so many with social anxieties and phobias of actual human interaction - absolutely! I don't think these people need an excuse, just a little grace and mercy. And I also think we should not be so quick to assume it's just a bunch of "millennials" who are spoiled or entitled. The main purpose for this book is to help others get to the point where they recognize many factors that contribute to why they struggle to accept themselves totally as they are. This must include us coming to terms with the fact that when we make assumptions about others, this judging them, (even when we think it's harmless or just being funny) that is because we also judge ourselves. We are super critical of our own persons so it's only natural that we would even in the most subtle ways do the same to others. It's just that often times we don't call it "judging" or making assumptions, we say things like "I'm just telling the truth" or "If this person REALLY wanted help, they'd start by getting off social media." There are plenty of other comments we make politely to ourselves that truthfully are us having a critical and skewed view of those around us. And I have seen more times than not, that is because we first view ourselves through that same lens.

Here's the thing, we are caught up in a world where we stick to our own little families, and our own circles. We are too busy for coffee or dinner with our close friends, or we choose to not make time for those things because of a wide variety of reasons that sound legit and valid to us. We work harder and get paid less, so when we are home we want to be with our family and relax. There are plenty who make time for social activities with people outside their circles, but in general we are less connected to others physically. Physically can mean calling people, not just seeing them face to face, but texting does not count. Yet we often do not even call our families or loved ones anymore because we say we don't know if they are busy, or whatever. I am just as guilty as the next person. I will admit, I do not like being on the actual phone. At the same time, it always makes my heart full when I do step out and talk to someone on the phone so I know I should make more time for this. It's amazing to me as I take notice of the people around me and those I know, the ones with a higher quality of life are spending more time face to face with friends and family. They are the ones who get on social media simply to check out other pictures, not to worry about showing off their own pictures even. They are the ones who have found more balance in this area of life, and it's usually pretty clear they are not the ones making subtle judgments about others. They aren't making comments that are negative about younger generations, or even those that are truly different from them. Overall their lives are more fulfilled and balanced, which shows most vividly through their in-person relationships.

AGAIN, I am somewhat of a social media junkie if you ask most, so this isn't me putting it down! This is me sharing what I have observed, and even noticed true within my own personal experience. I can honestly say that when I started getting to the internal place of self-acceptance, I

As I Am: Accepting Myself in an Unacceptable Society

noticed I judge less. I noticed I can scroll through Facebook and Instagram without thinking about all these goons posting crazy stuff. And for the better part of my normal, I can read something I disagree with passionately and not be offended by it or upset with it. We wonder why people are so easily offended these days; well I am going to tell you this - lack of physical communication has a huge part to play. It's not that suddenly people are headstrong about their opinions or beliefs, no. It's that because we sit in our own little worlds, with people in our circles who are similar minded as us, and we only keep what's different at a distance via social media, or what the television and news show us. We all know the biggest problem with technology is that it takes away the interpersonal skills we spent our childhood developing. We are losing the ability to interpret tone, and body language. We are never sure what humor people are using because too often we all take life much too seriously, and it seems that if we don't find humor in the same style as others, then someone is going to be put down for that too.

It's all a continuous cycle and the only way I can see it coming to a stop, is if we go back to learning how to start with ourselves. I believe we must open our inner eyes and begin to see how much we have lost our individuality in the rise of technology. We must begin to master balance so that we aren't so polarized in our thinking. Nothing is ever solely black or white. Even the Bible, that many of us believe states things clear, cut, and dry actually doesn't - if you want to know the TRUTH. Jesus' life's example should remind all how untrue it is to say the Bible says this or that and that's just it. If you read enough of it, you know that this is the very theology of the religious leaders in Jesus' day. Jesus talked in parables too, why? So the people would grasp the concepts of what He was teaching them. What is grace? In my opinion, it's the grey areas we all insist do not exist when it relates to something that ruffles our feathers of comfortability. If you want to love like "Jesus" or whoever you give thanks and pray to, you first must be willing to step outside your carnal, fallen nature. You first have to wake up and see your good, bad, ugly, and in between just as the one Creator sees it. You must be willing...

As I Am: Accepting Myself in an Unacceptable Society

I AM NOT BASHING SOCIAL MEDIA OR ENTERTAINMENT, I WANT TO MAKE PEOPLE AWARE, AND EXPRESS A SENSE OF BALANCING IS VITAL IF WE WANT TO EXPERIENCE LIFE CHANGE. BALANCE IS A LIFELINE IN ORDER TO FULL SELF-ACCEPTANCE AND SELF-LOVE.... BALANCE BALANCE BALANCE BALANCE!!!!!!!!!!!!!

Lists

Making lists was never one of my strong points. I make lists to remember my lists. Then I lose them or do not look at them. If I create them on an app or electronic device, I tend to not look at them. If I set them up with an alarm, I turn the alarm off, tell myself to check again when I am free, and usually end up distracted leaving them in the abyss of forgetfulness. However, sometimes God will tell me by ways of strongly nudging me internally to do what I normally have little success doing when it's in my own strength. During the summer of 2017, the one that changed my life as I had known it, I felt God nudging me to start making a very specific list. I felt like I needed to write down a list of things I liked about myself. However, I need to give you some back story first so let's put the idea of making lists off to the side for a minute.

Let me insert now that many people have always had this impression of me that I am this happy go-lucky, smiling person who never is down or depressed. That is often not the case. I have struggled with accepting and liking myself for many years now. I had more times than I could ever count where I felt completely lost, and very inadequate for life in general. This is an area very hard for me to admit, and I will add that much of it is because I allowed myself to listen to the opinions of others more than what I felt inside. I also tried too hard to fit into molds not designed for me. I always knew I was different and unique, but as I share throughout this book, you will learn I still struggle against TRULY loving and accepting me for me!

I was always better at seeing the positive in others' lives over my own. I had a knack for finding the silver lining in pretty much every single other person's life or situation except my own. And even when I would see the good things about myself, I had this bad habit of quickly reversing that when I made a mistake or when someone else got annoyed with me. Then this downward spiral of self-loathing and self-condemnation would happen. It would happen faster than lightning too. It wouldn't take long at all until I was in a very dark state of mind about how horrible or stupid, I was. I knew better too, and THAT made it all EVEN WORSE. Everything would somehow be my own doing, and I think part of this came from a place deep within me that always wanted to make sure I took ownership and responsibility for my own actions in life (a theme you should notice during this book; but AGAIN balance is the key). However, I am certain now that taking ownership or responsibility for your actions does not mean tearing yourself down like I did. I am sure if you are reading this you can relate and like me you tend to be much more critical of yourself than you need to be. Let me remind you, it is not noble or honorable. It is not attractive at all, and it does not look fancy on anyone. True self love and full acceptance of oneself is much more beautiful and handsome on all who wear it.

This was something that had to change for me. This was something I knew I had to overcome if I was going to stop the cycle I was living in. The cycle of believing, *"This was just the story of my life,"* to get up in life to have my feet knocked out from under me! That I was just DOOMED to live in a constant sense of resistance to the GOOD LIFE. I was in this cycle that I felt I would get ahead in life or heck even just catch up, and then suddenly out of nowhere, it seemed, I would get slammed with some obstacle that pushed me back. Suddenly it seemed like things would always come at me that undid all the progress I felt I was making. Truly ironic because even the actual process to write this book has been a plethora of odd obstacles, and even more than usual for me!

I began writing this book the last week in January 2018, and I have one super cool story of how I believe God confirmed to me REPEARTEDLY that I was on POINT (but you will just have to stick around to hear about THAT, it's for another time). Around October 2018, 10 months later I was ¾ of the way through with the book. The journey to this point alone has been faced with a laundry list of hurdles, including 2 serious surgeries, my son also had emergency surgery, we moved, had 2 totaled cars within 6 month's time, and that's just the BIG stuff. Oy Vei! Had I tried to write this in my past years, I would not be at this point after 10 months. I would have thrown in the towel and walked away from the dream. Timing is usually not my strong suit. HOWEVER, in that exact same sense, I now CAN look over and see that it's not supposed to be! Why? Because God's timing is not ours! Yea, sounds cliché, I know, I know. But honestly, it's insane how I can see it all connecting! By the middle of 2019 while I was editing and reviewing this and working with a publisher, I was still facing obstacles that my old nature would have given up! I AM STILL pushing forward!! Often, the very things that seem like they are meant to take you out, are the very reasons YOU KEEP PUSHING FORWARD!!! They become the actual obstacles that build your character, strength, and make you the person you dreamed of being and never ever thought you could be!

I really believe perspective makes all the difference of course, and it took me 35 years, my son graduating early, my second marriage failing (really just coming to an end because failure is the wrong word), my church at the time closing, and the fact that I was 3 semesters away from my Bachelors degree unable to finish because of financial reasons - for me to realize that I had to do something, and something DRASTICALLY DIFFERENT than I had tried repeatedly. Something completely left from what I always THOUGHT was "right".

I would like to note that I had gone to college on and off from 2004 till 2016. In 2013 I finally got my associates degree, and when I got married in 2016, we were going through a custody battle for my 5-year-old stepson, so I decided that needed my full attention. It just so happened I was at the end of my financial aid as well because I did not steward my last 3 semesters properly. I literally remember feeling like my entire life was all a lost cause. I remember that was this summer, 2017, when I honestly believed everything I stood for was questioned. Everything I believed I was working for was wrong, and that I was at my mental and emotional rock bottom. I mentioned this in the beginning of the book. It was this summer and the months to follow that birthed this book...

Now back to the nudging for me to make that list of things I liked about myself....

When I feel God nudging me about something, there are times I second guess myself, and He tends to repeat what He is wanting me to do. It's like this tugging feeling deep within me that I cannot ignore too long or

I will go a little insane. I'm just saying. I already didn't like making lists. I would much rather just talk out loud to myself or anyone else for that matter to just avoid creating a list about ANYTHING. And here I needed to write down what I liked about myself. I had to write down things I liked that people may not have liked, and this was difficult for me because I felt like I shouldn't put those things on the list. I spent so many years fighting with myself over this one thing. If I am totally transparent with you, I still struggle a little with this area too. I spent years believing if other people did not like something about me, physically or personality wise, then it was something I too should view as "wrong with me". Maybe not wrong with me, but I felt as if I SHOULD NO WAY think it positive or likable. Well, here I was facing myself with God; having a conversation something like this:

God: [Conversation with God #1] "Danielle, I want you to sit down and write a list of all the things you like about yourself. I don't want you to over think this either, just write…"

Me: "Okay, I can do that…. Well, I like my hair. I have great hair, even though I tend to complain about it on days I don't feel like messing with it. Well, I guess I shouldn't do that, you know complain about it. I mean some people really don't have good hair. HAHAHA This is silly, my mother always told me that was part of why she liked my father- HE HAD GREAT HAIR. Ugh, okay… I need to think. I like my smile, and I guess I have decent teeth. I do enjoy laughing, and I generally am easily amused. I like that about myself. I am easy to entertain. I am easy to please......."

God: "Really?? Easy to please... That's interesting. Do you realize what you literally just wrote down? In the same sentence you said you liked your hair,

but yet you still complain about it. Often.... And then you said you are easily pleased? I am not sure you understand what you are saying. I will be quiet till you THINK you are done...."

Me: "Well, I made a mistake. It's just a bad habit cause I don't want people to think I am vain about my hair. I don't MEAN to complain about it. OKAY well back to my list. I really like that I can talk with most anyone I meet about anything at all even when its something I don't know too much about. I think that's great and comes in handy. Well, as long as I don't get carried away and off topic, then it's not really great. Then people think I am some type of know it all. So I don't know. I like that and I don't. HA, I know something, I really love that I have totally been through all kinds of crazy weird stuff! That makes me unique and different! Makes me stand out and I always have some funny freaking story to share. Well, then again people don't really like that either because they think I am making shit up. (Yes, I say shit when I talk to God). That's so irritating though that people are forever judging me without getting to know me just cause I share funny stories related to the topic brought up. I guess I don't really like that. OH! I love that I have this way about me of being really captivating and talking very animated. I like that one! Mostly. Well, I do until people tell me I am too loud, or think I am yelling at them, or tell me they are too distracted to pay attention cause it looks like I am throwing gang signs talking with my hands... Well, maybe I could sit on my hands more or fold them or DO SOMETHING besides talk WITH them.... I mean it doesn't bother me, but apparently anyone within arm's reach may feel violated or distracted.... Maybe they just have untreated ADD!"

"I like that usually I am right when discerning situations or calling things out before they happen! That has been helpful. A I OT!!!. Ugh, but that's another one of those things I think is a blessing and a curse because again people think I am being some "know it all" or I don't know what their deal is, but I only speak up when I am asked and then of course it will backfire."

"You know what I don't really think this is a good time for this right now God. I will do this another day, because all the things I thought I liked about myself remind me how much everyone else hates them about me. So I just rather not do this right now. All these things that I think might be even a smidge special, someone always critiques or comments about how annoying it is. OR reminds me how much I do it. I mean pretty much all the things I think I like about myself are basically all the things everyone else can't stand. So YEA Not a good time. .... This is making me feel worse by the minute because seriously if MULTIPLE PEOPLE, different people are saying the SAME THINGS than I am pretty sure I AM THE COMMON DENOMINATOR. THANKS GOD BUT NO THANKS, NOT RIGHT NOW!"

God: "Danielle.... You aren't listening to me........."

Me: "YES I AM! IT'S JUST STUPID AND I DON'T HAVE TIME TO DO THIS RIGHT NOW. I AM STRESSED ENOUGH ABOUT ALL THE CRAP I DO WRONG. I DON'T NEED TO SIT AND WRITE IT ALL DOWN! I DON'T WANT

TO WRITE DOWN WHAT I LIKE ABOUT MYSELF BECAUSE IT'S ALL THE THINGS EVERYONE HATES ABOUT ME. OR IF THEY DON'T HATE THEM, THEY AT LEAST REMIND ME HOW THESE ARE THINGS THAT ARE NOT POSITIVE things and I am INSANE for liking them. OR TEASE ME WITHOUT CEASING ABOUT THEM! SO WHY SHOULD I LIKE THEM IF THEY FREAKING BOTHER. EVERY DANG ELSE AROUND ME ESPECIALLY THE PEOPLE I LOVE?"

God: "You are still not listening to me, but I can clearly tell you are upset, so go get some rest and we will continue this another time. I am not done with this though. But you need to calm yourself, and just be still.... Goodnight my beautiful, my love..."

Me: "Yea I guess... Beautiful, psh thanks. Your love? You know I really don't understand that. I don't see how you love me when supposedly YOU created me the way I am, yet the same crap always happens. People always complain about the very things I like about me. Ugh whatever...."

As I Am: Accepting Myself in an Unacceptable Society

This continues, but I wanted to break this up a little. This is a great time to insert a doodle spot or one of our interactive things. Something that is less serious and more playful like a coloring doodle.

As I Am: Accepting Myself in an Unacceptable Society

These conversations between me and God sometimes end in me reverting to that very dark place I mentioned earlier on. I need to say they did so because I was NOT using a clear perspective! I wouldn't BE STILL. I allowed the voices of others override God and what I felt deep down. I usually got extremely flustered, but during this time, the summer of 2017, I was pretty much at my end. I was basically at this point not wanting to carry this conversation on. I would feel the nudge in me when I would be quietly reading or studying something. I would avoid it. You know, now that I think about it, I don't think I sat back down to finish this list or conversation with God for months to come. There were many conversations, prayer time, one sided yelling fits (from me towards Him), and countless amounts of tear-filled eyes. I am certain I could have filled any local LAKE by the end of that summer! Night after night I cried myself to sleep during the months that followed in 2017. But something else also was happening during this time. Something that came in small doses, and I had to work hard to notice. I was recreating myself. I was allowing myself to redefine what I wanted for my life. I was having these moments of joy, and true freedom. They were hard to see at first because I was still so upset and angry. I was still so unsure of what I liked about myself. I still couldn't bring myself to finish that conversation with God, nor finish my list.

What amuses me the most is when I looked back over my journal, I noticed pages I wrote that contained small positive things I would talk about. I noticed little things here and there that I wrote about describing things I liked about myself. Or at least things about myself I was coming to a healthier internal view of. My perspective was taking small baby steps in a new direction right before me. Right amid all these tears and angry tantrums!

Then I remember picking up an old journal of mine that said SMILE on the cover. I opened it up and inside I had written pages of what looked to be 1 continual list! HA! A list I wrote, AND continued? This amused and confused me at the same time because I had totally forgotten about it! It was a journal I wrote only things I was thankful for, and things that brought me joy. This journal is in storage now, so I am not sure the years I wrote in it, but it was definitely over the course of several years, and each and every page was full of short statements about the things that I was thankful for. This brought tears to my eyes. The GOOD KIND of tears!! And I was ready to finish that conversation with God about the list of things I liked about myself. I also knew it was time to face what I was denying and running from.

This is important for you to read, so I am going to type out that conversation like before:

Me: "Alright Daddy. I'm ready. I know I have been stubborn, and I have been angry with you. I don't understand so many things anymore and I am really still disappointed that I am actually not as self-accepting as I thought I was. YEARS! I spent years undoing toxic abuse, and I truly thought I was sooooooooooooo much farther than clearly, I was- in loving myself for real. I am also really sorry for acting so much like a complete brat."

God: "I love you more than you can imagine. I love you, and it's OKAY."

In that moment, I could literally feel the presence of love surrounding me. I could honestly feel as if I was being held.

"Now... You say that you're ready. Are you going to listen to Me before you start talking this time? Are you going to listen when I hush you because you are missing the point? Are you REALLY READY to listen to Me???"

Me: ".......SIGH...... Yes. I am ready to listen. Actually listen. I am ready to be still."

God: "Good. Now then, I want you to write a list of what YOU like about yourself. I don't want you to tell me what YOU THINK others think of the things YOU LIKE. I am asking you to make a list of things YOU LIKE. THINGS YOU FIND VALUE in about YOURSELF. I am asking you to be STILL. Shut out the voices of others. Shut out what you THINK is vain or wrong or good or not. I am not asking for your judgments. I am asking you to write down WHAT YOU LIKE ABOUT YOU. Nothing more, nothing less. This is not about anybody else. NOT about what you sound like or should say or shouldn't. JUST WHAT YOU LIKE. DO you get it? DO YOU think you can do this now???"

Me: "I can. I just need to be quiet for a little bit...."

As I Am: Accepting Myself in an Unacceptable Society

I put on my favorite worship music list. I was quiet. I took slow, deep breathes in. And exhaled even slower. I closed my eyes while feeling the air on my face, hearing the instruments playing in the worship music. I would intentionally have to quiet my thoughts to only picture God as I do when I pray. I picture a loving, strong father who mostly was just bright, JUST LIKE the sun beaming on my face on the most beautiful spring afternoon! Tears were shed, but this time they were because I knew I was in the presence of my Creator. I was surrounded by a force much greater than myself. Yet, a force that made me feel completely safe and at peace. I felt that from within me. I felt God from the very depths of my every cell, even to my bone marrow! From the inside radiating outwardly, wrapping love around me. I remembered I was created and designed with a very unique and distinct purpose. I was all the things I was for a reason. Every single last thing... The good, the bad, the ugly, and everything in between. EVERYTHING!!!!!!!!

Me: "List of things I like about myself; I know a lot of random information about all types of topics and can keep up with, or definitely follow along with almost any conversation I am involved in. I have been through a lot of stuff in my life, and therefore I have a wide variety of life experiences that often others do not have at my age. I am able to sense things about people and situations that many times others cannot. I observe what isn't always seen, I hear what isn't usually heard. I pay attention to things beneath the obvious. I talk a lot when I am passionate about the topic. I talk with my hands and I can make myself laugh easily. I am kindhearted even when others are not... I genuinely look for the good in everyone, even people who do ungodly things. I want to help everyone I meet, even if they think I am a looney toon. I like the fact that I am transparent with people because I want them to feel they can relate to me. I like that people often feel understood by me. I like that I can laugh at myself, and NORMALLY I am not too easily offended. I like that I can forget stuff I did 5 minutes ago, that comes in handy when I am mad or upset. LOL."

God: "HEY Wait a minute. What happened to all the physical traits you listed last time? Why are none of those being mentioned?"

Me: "Well, that's because those don't matter as much. I still like those things, and some I still struggle with worrying what others think. But what I learned most while being quiet is that the things that many people can't stand about me are the very things I actually do like. Even the things that often annoy myself."

The list was actually longer, and this conversation had a few more joking moments between me and The Big Guy in the sky, however, I think I made my point. When God asked me to make a list of things I liked about myself, at first it made me ridiculously uncomfortable. I don't exactly like making lists to begin with, but it was really hard for me to not allow what other people had told me or usually said about me affect what I liked about myself. I honestly spent many evenings fighting with myself over this one task. I can remember writing things and then scratching them out, and it was as if God was sitting on one shoulder and the devil on the other. I would write something. Then the devil would remind me of how many times someone said that thing was bad about me, so I would scratch it out. Then the side with God on it would say, "But this other person over here, this 1 person told you how much they appreciated that about you so don't scratch that out."

As I Am: Accepting Myself in an Unacceptable Society

It was something kind of out of the cartoons honestly. Nearly everything that I WROTE I felt a tug in both directions over, the enemy would name off 3-5 people or more who confirmed the negative view, and then God would usually name 1 single person who confirmed the positive view. However, I began to see the pattern God was wanting me to see. He was reminding me that just like I believe His Son Jesus died on the cross for the 1, the Me; He would leave the 99 to go after the 1. Just like that, if those traits about myself offended 10 people and caused them to hate me - there was always at least 1 whom that very same attribute helped in greater ways that absolutely outweighed a zillion people disliking it. It all had a purpose! My quirky tendencies and life experiences had purpose. I was, nope...I AM designed to reach a very needed and yet very diverse tribe of people. There are reasons far greater than I could ever see with my human finite vision for every weird thing about myself, and every life experience I have walked through. I had a story to share. I have A LOT of stories to share. I have a perspective that even if only 1 would resonate with, they needed me to be me. All of me. I was designed with a purpose beyond what I could comprehend.

As I Am: Accepting Myself in an Unacceptable Society

So make a list. Write down things about yourself you know. What I learned from this was that the first list tends to have all types of things on it. Things I liked and didn't like, things I wasn't sure of even. Things that you like will begin to surface the more you go through this list. Work on the list a few minutes every day for a good week if you are diligent. If you're more like me take a few weeks, but STICK WITH WORKING ON IT. Be CONSISTENT. You can add things you don't care for as well but keep them separate. Maybe put the positive on one side of the paper and negative on the other. Remember though it isn't a competition so this list doesn't have to have equal things on both sides, maybe I am the only one, but my tendency for balance can often be imbalanced! The list for like and dislike isn't meant to be "balanced". With that being said, I want to encourage you that if you look over the lists, and you notice the dislike side has more things - begin to dig a little deeper for positive. Ideally, we want to get the positive list to outshine the negative. It's helpful to write all you can think of that can be put into words. This will not only give you a better gauge of what areas you could work on, but it will show you how many wonderful things there are about you.

As I Am: Accepting Myself in an Unacceptable Society

Part of the problem in our society is that we are taught if we talk about ourselves in positive ways, we are viewed negatively. This just isn't true, and it breaks my heart to know many of us walk around constantly feeling guilty for genuinely having positive things about ourselves we like. There really is a distinct difference in self-confidence and genuine self-love versus self-absorption and self-centeredness. Somewhere our society has seemed to blur these lines, leaving so many of us carrying false guilt and shame over something vital to living a full, healthy, and happy life.

As you are working on this, remember my story. Do not sit there and make a list based on what YOU THINK others like. At the same time do not write stuff down thinking despite what others have said either. You write down things YOU LIKE, things YOU KNOW about yourself that you truly like. It might start off that your list is of physical traits, and that's okay. Just please keep in mind this is meant to go beyond that. This is meant to help move you into a place where you can begin to see yourself in a new light. We will work on other lists too, but at this moment it's important that we raise your own awareness of how likable and acceptable you truly are. Right now we are being intentional. If we don't know what we like about ourselves we will continue to listen to the many voices around us telling us all sorts of things, that just aren't usually correct. Most of the time it's other's opinions, which varies based on their perspectives, and their own life filters. I want to insert a note here;

Every single person has their own hurts and habits that shape their perspective no matter how similar to you in personality or how similar life circumstances they share. I think we all tend to completely ignore this. It doesn't matter what we have in common with others, everyone was raised in different environments, with different family traditions and cultures. Every single person has had their own share of some form of troubled times or painful experiences that shape their thinking and their opinions. Everyone's filter for the world, and themselves is going to be different, with various contributing factors.

As I Am: Accepting Myself in an Unacceptable Society

INTERACTION TIME

I Am affirmation Word Search

t o l e q e c a h v m o a t l

h q q o k w l o c g h u y o u

a e o p v i y i m e u h i j f

n l o g v e t n a p a o g d i

k b w e y n d l s n l x n n t

f a c c e p t e d t f e p e u

u t b h f h y h t r o w t x a

l s t k y e p o h u i w v e e

d u b g i w b r z t m y e h b

a p h e a l e d s h q a h l l

As I Am: Accepting Myself in an Unacceptable Society

WORD BANK

accepted	healthy	alive	hope
authentic	loved	beautiful	stable
complete	thankful	enough	truth
healed	worthy		

As I Am: Accepting Myself in an Unacceptable Society

I want to inspire you to take journaling more seriously if you don't already do it. It's not only beneficial for you to write down positive characteristics about yourself, it is also a way to clear some mental space for yourself. I think it's important to live our lives intentionally and that isn't something taught often. It also isn't something that is a natural habit for most of us. However, if I can adopt this practice, you most definitely can. I believe in YOU! Have a journal you write only things positive like things you are thankful for. Write things in that journal that lift you up, and make you smile no matter how small or insignificant it may seem. These types of journals are very helpful when you are having one of those rough days where you just feel down in general. It's also a helpful idea to have another journal for self-reflection and working on getting to know yourself more intimately. Maybe just start with a journal that has sections. I am a writer so it's easy for me to write and I need separate journals. If you must, recreate some parts of yourself, redefine things using new words; maybe write yourself little notes about areas you want to strive for if you need to. Sometimes I have found along my journey that I have to remodel different areas within myself. For me, as long as I do it with God, the remodeling doesn't take as long and isn't nearly as painful as having everything blow up in my face like when stuck in the cycle. Nor does it cause us to be in complete emotional despair when we allow a power greater rise within us to guide and direct in this internal remodeling. Some remodeling examples I did were switching over to new healthier habits like eating more to fuel myself and not comfort eating or eating for pure pleasure. I also began to view my exercise habits differently which helped me stick to these new habits with consistency. Remodeling myself just meant I had to view these areas in myself with a different view so that I found purpose to form these new habits. I had to learn how to truly value these new things. When we see the value in something, it makes it a whole lot easier to follow through.

It is important to list the things you don't care for as well, but please, PLEASE remember the focus is not to feel worse about yourself, but to face these areas with new perspective. So it is important to keep in mind that you must not over think the list of stuff you don't care for or the list of traits you know need work. I have written down things like "I say words wrong too frequent, I do not spell check, I run over curbs," etc. I brought in a lot of my little annoyances for this area because sometimes we do not actually realize how much these little things do affect the way we think or view ourselves. So again, EVERYTHING counts. And this is not something you have to do overnight. It is something to do whenever you feel like you need to, or when you are ready to; AT YOUR OWN PACE. It is important though to face and openly write or admit the things you don't like. It's important so those areas can lose their power over you; SO they can no longer cause you to feel subconsciously insecure about them. Once you admit something openly to yourself like we talked about in the denial chapter, those things lose their grip. Then they will not pop their head up in defense randomly out of nowhere! Well, they may try, but I can assure you it will be less and less as each day, week, month, and year passes. This is about shifting your mindset. It's a lifestyle change. It's thinking with intention. Living on purpose.

Listing your traits, all of them, also helps you track your growth and gives you feedback that is healthy. If you don't like yourself, how do you expect anyone else to? If you don't treat yourself with respect, how do you think others will treat you? Sure this isn't the rule for everyone, but for the majority it really is. Others treat us based on what and how we allow them to. I promise you, subconsciously you are showing those around you how to treat you based on HOW YOU INTERNALLY perceive yourself! Key is subconsciously, hence why many of us do not even realize it.

Make a list of things you like about yourself. Make a list of things you don't like. Make a list of things you are indifferent about. Find out more about yourself. Make a list of your fears. You see, God nudged me to make this first list of things I liked about myself, but as I did, I felt the nudge to keep making these new lists. I hate lists remember! I don't make LISTS! Not hardly even for grocery shopping! I have improved though and found so much greatness in this little tool! Lists for me are difficult to keep concise, but I make them anyway when I need to. This also works for working on finding what it is you're passionate about! I keep starting my bucket list, but I never finish it and I keep losing it! That's what happens when I don't mark my journal pages, and I do write in several journals at once. Oh WELL! I have also worked on lists of places I want to visit, and things I would like to do. I think this helps us set goals for ourselves easier, along with there being a little secret power in writing stuff down and seeing it often. You will find out that when you do this, you will eventually begin looking for ways to enhance the positive and achieve the things you write down. It's similar to the purpose of vision boards! Those are really great tools as well! That's basically take a list and using pictures to represent the words! It's more my type of list to make, mostly because I love making collages. I get to make messes with pictures and rearrange them a zillion times. I get to change my mind, add pictures, take some away, and just basically let creativity freely flow! I want to encourage you to be creative once this becomes a more comfortable exercise for you! You can make lists of positive words you would like to incorporate more often in your vocabulary. Lists don't have to be daunting, and that is still a struggle for me to keep in mind. They are a very useful tool to help me be more intentional in any area of my life. They are tools that can bring out traits within me I didn't realize this because I never stopped to intentionally define myself through creating a simple list as a guide. Lists serve many purposes; use them to help you achieve your goals and be the person you were truly created to be. Do not allow them to hold a negative, scary connotation. Do not allow yourself to make a list only with the purpose of crossing things off it. That is only one use for them, and while it is an extremely productive way to get things done, it limits the way we can benefit from these little beauties.

Start simple. Then add on and continue building your lists! Help switch your perspective by putting specific with your lists! Intentional thinking leads to intentional living! When we live on purpose, we can experience more of life's abundant joy because we leave less to chance or luck. We can learn through being intentional how it leads to becoming more adaptable as well. Being adaptable is so important, but we will save that for another book, for now let's keep working on accepting ourselves as we are.

My List...

_____

_____

_____

_____

_____

_____

_____

_____

_____

_____

_____

_____

_____

_____

_____

_____

_____

_____

_____

_____

_____

_____

_____

_____

_____

_____

_____

_____

_____

_____

As I Am: Accepting Myself in an Unacceptable Society

Guilt & Shame

"Shame is a focus on self, guilt is a focus on behavior. Shame is, "*I am bad.*" Guilt is, "*I did something bad.*" How many of you, if you did something that was hurtful to me, would be willing to say, "*I'm sorry. I made a mistake?*" How many of you would be willing to say that? Guilt: "*I'm sorry. I made a mistake.*" Shame: "*I'm sorry. I am a mistake.*"

-Brene Brown-

[https://fs.blog/2014/10/brene-brown-guilt-shame/]

The quote used to open this chapter is from the brilliant researcher at the University of Houston, Dr. Brene Brown. I used another quote earlier in the book from her book "Braving the Wilderness," and when I read this comment again off of a TED talk, I believe she did, I was reminded how much she inspired me when writing this. I have only read one of her books so far, but I have a list I plan to read asap. Yes, lol, a list.

As I Am: Accepting Myself in an Unacceptable Society

SIDE NOTE: I feel like I need to add the fact that the majority of my life I was not one who typically read for "fun". My mother was a very avid reader and encouraged me to pick it up over my childhood, but I was just too busy. I was busy playing outside, or pretending I was some amazing dance performer, or even better, that I was yes, a motivational speaker teaching people how to make the best of their seemingly crappy lives. (I was a kid y'all. I seriously wanted to help people make their lives better as long as I can remember and it's pretty funny to me thinking about it.) As an adult I was always having to read for college, so I definitely did not want to read for "fun".

I can tell you - reading, even when I have had to somewhat force myself to do so, has been one of the most influencing and beneficial habits I have trained myself to do. Now I love it. I still must be honest and tell you I don't really read fiction; I read non-fiction. Books that will inspire me and help me to grow. I want to change that, but for now it's something I encourage everyone to do more of in their personal lives.

BACK TO BRENE BROWN'S BOOKS: I promise you, reading her books or even just listening to her speak will not disappoint you. She dives far deeper into some of the topics I have discussed, and she gets a little more technical while keeping the material relatable. This topic is a doozy for so many of us because we carry both guilt & shame often without even recognizing it. Guilt can be a good thing to an extent, but when we carry false guilt or guilt that we no longer need to be carrying, then it easily turns into anxiety and all sorts of negative feelings within ourselves. I will get more in depth about shame in this chapter, but for the moment I first want to address guilt, along with how often it's falsely imposed by our biggest enemy, ourselves. Which by the way, taking the steps to accept and love yourself in a new, more intimate authentic way is the absolute sure beginning to the end of you being your worst enemy!

False guilt is something I never paid much attention to until a pastor I had brought it up when counseling me on some areas. Like I said, I have read so many self-help books, and studied psychology, and gone to Celebrate Recovery, etc., yet here I was struggling so much with this nagging feeling like I had something to feel bad for. As if I did something wrong or said something wrong. I have tried to analyze this to find out where precisely the tendency came from. Honestly though I don't think there is a PRECISE factor. I am sure it's a multitude of them. I have always been a fan of the concept saying, "If you find the root and address that, the issue will dissipate," but I am learning that often it isn't just one root. And when it comes to the psyche and emotions within our bodies, it isn't layered like an onion, although that is a pretty accurate description; thanks Shrek!

In my viewpoint, it is more likely the root system under a massively huge oak tree. And of course the older we are, or the more "life weathering" we have gone through, the deeper, thicker, more intertwined root system there is. This makes things annoying for myself. I am the type of person

I want to know where a tendency is coming from, address that, and move on. Yea, well life doesn't work like that, so I have to get over it. HA. Alright so you are probably thinking you could care less about the mumbo jumbo of why or how something came about, let's just find the solution. I agree, however, this is one of those areas that if you are not careful you will just place a band-aid over the issue and continue on only to find out it ends up getting worse. You will wake up one day with all these heart issues, and physical illnesses that are from "stress," yet you sit there thinking you aren't stressed. Not stressed like once upon a time in your life at least, so why suddenly now? Guilt does that. Especially false guilt that you place a temporary fix over in order to simply not deal with it yet. Which I laugh at myself as I write this because I know half of the time, the guilt I am feeling isn't even true guilt so what am I so afraid of? Why don't I just address it to find out if it's even valid?

Annnnnd here it comes; afraid that I may have to face the fact that I am not living up to some standard or expectation someone else placed on me. Afraid that I just may be wrong and have to relearn a new way of thinking about something. Afraid that I might ACTUALLY have all those horrible ugly traits others told me I did, or even just ONE of them. Some days it is just easier to hide from even the false guilt, because we simply get paralyzed by the WHAT IFs, the fear that all the lies we believe just might be true. I have a little secret though, even if you are not the most moral person on earth, even if you are not very thoughtful or concerned for others, even if you are a little self-absorbed and inconsiderate, YOU ARE NOT DEFINED BY THAT!

At least you do not have to be. So let's keep the momentum going. Let's talk about the differences in false guilt, true guilt, and shame. Let me share with you my journey of how these issues factor into true self-acceptance, and more importantly how they can be life shifters for you! You see, the very things usually designed to take us out tend to be the catalyst that shoot us right to the stars! Remember, this is a journey to YOUR SELF ACCEPTANCE. YOUR GENUINE, AUTHENTIC SELF ACCEPTANCE AND UNCONDITIONAL SELF LOVE.

This is meant to challenge you, push you out of your internal comfort zone just enough to motivate you towards actions steps. This is a guide to lead your life into a 180 degree turn for the better, helping you to live a life of abundance, love, and prosperity, exposing you to life that has been shut out because of limiting belief systems intended to keep you from reaching your full potential. We only get one life you guys, and we honestly do have the choice of what that life will be. It does not matter what circumstances you were or are in. I know that for a fact from experience, as well as the hundreds of amazingly wealthy, successful others out there who turned their life around to be greater than what it was or should have been. They all started their journey within themselves. They all started within the context of their own internal story, and their internal view. They started with themselves as you are doing. SO take a few minutes to soak in what you've read thus far. Stretch your limbs a tad, and maybe get a glass of wine or water. Take some deep long breaths and come on with me into the ugly part of self we know as guilt and shame…. Color the cocoon image and think about the transformation of the caterpillar turning into a beautiful butterfly. While it's in the cocoon phase it's getting rid of the old exterior, what used to be its form. Understanding more about the differences between guilt and shame are actually very similar. It helps us transform from what we once were, into what we can become! During this time, we may need to separate or distant ourselves from others. This isn't meant to isolate or alienate though, it is so we can truly allow ourselves some space for mental clarity. This way we can get rid of what no longer NEEDS to be part of us. You know that old saying, you can't see the forest through the trees? Whatever it says, it means if you are standing in the middle of chaos you usually can't clearly SEE it for what is REALLY

IS. THAT is what we want! We want to see ourselves for WHO we really

ARE, ALL OF OURSELVES. The good, the bad, the ugly, and

ALLLLLLLLLLLLLLLLLLL the in between!

As I Am: Accepting Myself in an Unacceptable Society

If I were to ask you if you knew the difference between false and true, you would more than likely tell me, "DUH"... True and false are opposites, one means it is accurate or real and the other means it is not real, it is not correct. I want to encourage you to stay aware that this is not about right or wrong. You see, in today's society we have a tendency of labeling stuff right or wrong, good or bad, and from that we judge. I don't believe we all do it intentionally, it's just how most of us were taught. However, when I say stay aware, it's important to differentiate the true context and meaning of words in their actual context. Because right and wrong to most of us means automatically that its good or bad. That simply isn't true though.

To be honest with all our technology communication these days, I believe context has been so forgotten and is a key source as to why there seems to be an epidemic of miscommunication. You could tell me it's "wrong" to say the sky is green because it's blue. You wouldn't be incorrect because clearly the sky is not green it is generally blue (unless you are color blind). But something rises up in me when someone tells me I am "wrong", and I get this sudden desire to say something like,

As I Am: Accepting Myself in an Unacceptable Society

"How can you tell me it's wrong to say the sky is green, if I think the sky is green I can. You aren't the sky police." DO you sense that sudden tone of defensiveness? However, if you told me, "It's incorrect," or, "It's false to say the sky is green," I might be less likely to come back at you defensively. So as you read, I would like you to not see false as bad, wrong as negative, etc. This is something that if you practice it will become easier and second nature for you to stop judging yourself and even others. We don't want to see ourselves that way, but it's what happens. It's what we do without thinking about it. If you tell me I am WRONG, I think you are telling me I am bad for whatever it is. Or I feel like I am suddenly inadequate because I am WRONG... It's nonsense to me now, but I still must check myself.

SO when I say something is false, or not true please don't be quick to start thinking it's bad. Just as much as if I say something is true, it does not mean it is good. And I guess I must also go on to say that EVEN IF something is bad, it doesn't make YOU or the one who did it a bad person! I want to quote something out of a book I read that I just thought to be greatness. It is also something I want to write out on a giant poster and hang in my creative space at home because it is THAT worthy of remembering....

Seth Godin wrote it in his book called Tribes (pg. 108),

"The secret of being wrong isn't to avoid being wrong! The secret is being willing to be wrong. The secret is realizing that wrong isn't fatal. The only thing that makes people and organizations great is their willingness to be NOT great along the way."

In order for us to change how we view ourselves, we really have to see some of these mindless habits for what they are. They have to be brought up so we can recognize them. I am serious when I say that most of the world is so darn offended all the time because we have lost the sense of context in our communication. We also have to stop labeling stuff! I understand the value of "labels." I use them myself, but to serve a purpose, not define character from them. You can wear a name tag that says "Mom" or "Dad" - that's a label; or even better, how about "role"? Are you solely defined by that one label??????????? Nope. At least not any moms or dads I know. That label, title, or role is only a portion of what defines that person's character, a piece of the whole person. I personally group people using labels or their roles because of the commonalities shared with others. Brown haired girls, blonde hair girls. Moms groups, single mom groups. My fellow ADD/ADHDer's. There are things people within each label or role can relate to with one another that mostly others outside of that cannot. At least not in the same way. SIDE NOTE: To me I would say our titles or roles are when we say moms, dads, siblings, employees, etc. Labels would be more like the adjectives used to describe something about us such as brown hair, blue eyes, our ethnicity would fit here in my opinion too, as well as our sexual preferences (which really should not be anyone's business, but it is what it is in our society). I'm explaining this because it helps clarify the different levels at which labels can be used in a non-negative way, and labels are not exactly the same as the roles we play, though they both get us grouped, and stereotyped. They both cause a disconnect among humanity and do not have to.

For that reason, society has tended to group people to assist with research. The heart of grouping people according to "labels" was not always meant to single people out or cause division to the point of segregation. You must hear that THE HEART of it was intended to build community and bring us closer with others WHO SHARED COMMON THINGS WITH US.

You have to see past what our tendencies are because of the society we live in now, which is to only see how it has negatively affected us. Census was once used to help determine the needs of communities and served other positive reasoning behind it. It was not just to say, "Hey! This area has more minorities than this one," or whatever; PERSPECTIVE is such a life changer...

There is nothing wrong with taking pride in a "label" or some commonality you share with others, but we must first DECIDE how we will choose to use them. We MUST learn to redefine the context in which we use the word, and how we think about it. When I tell you to stop labeling, I mean do not use a label to solely define a person, including yourself. BALANCE FOLKS, LIFE IS ABOUT FINDING A BALANCE!!!!

I am not defined by the fact that I have an ADD brain, but that is technically a label. In truth though, I love knowing that "label" because it helps me connect with others who share things with me many will not ever relate to. It has also helped me understand more about myself, and how my brain tends to function. BUT I do not use that label as an excuse for my undesirable behaviors. I do use it to refer to how I think so that others can hopefully be more gracious when I repeat myself 10 times and then say, "Sorry, I am ADD and it's taking me longer to process or soak in what was said." That is not an excuse! It is also not me explaining myself. You know, that's another soap box I could get on! I understand that I have the tendency to over explain to people and it comes from years of living a life trying to please others because I was starving for acceptance.

However, these days I don't explain myself because I care what others think of me. I explain AT TIMES, so people can be more aware of how I am, and where I'm coming from. I really think this is another thing that gets a negative connotation and it has caused me some unnecessary damage internally. YET OF COURSE the minute you don't explain something a little more to someone, then they say, "Well you could just give me a little additional information, so I know better how to take you or how to better help you."

YEA RIGHT SHUT IT, I ATTEMPTED TO PERSON!!!!!!!!! (told you-soapbox ha)

I mean this shouldn't be such a big deal, but in my journey it seems as if people are so stinking used to people over explaining that they stop paying full attention to even see if what the person is telling them is helpful to building a better relationship with the other. I strongly feel we are so darn quick to start labeling and judging people simply from the words used in a few sentences. Stop and pay attention. Watch people when you talk to them, be aware of your immediate thoughts as people talk to you. TEST IT OUT. TRY it and see.

We must build a foundation of what truth is and what false is at its very simplistic level before we can add them to describing something as disabling as guilt (bet you forgot we were talking about guilt to begin with). Think about the times you ended up in an argument with someone and in the end, you found out that there was actually nothing to be arguing about to begin with. The problem is that we are living in a tech world where shorthand lingo such as K or LOL has taken the bulk of our small talk. So much so that when we are in actual conversations with people, we are either too impatient to listen all the way through, or we have lost much of our social skills because we have hid behind our screens simply texting. It is time we address this LOUDLY and CLEARLY!

This isn't just for the younger generations folks. I am almost 37 years old, and I see it every single day in people of every generation. Most of us are walking around feeling "some kind of way" over something we conjured up within our own minds, simply because we do not practice the art of communication and interpersonal skills nearly as often as we once did collaboratively. Too many do not realize how technology is breaking down the way we relate and interact with one another, and it has left so many of us guessing or assuming what others say and mean. We need to take this seriously and we need to remember there is a way to have our technology and interpersonal skills too! The result of this behavior leaves people turning inward to understand others through their own filter. Life filter is just what it says. It's how we filter life's experiences, and all that we have to process. If my life filter is one of positivity, then all I take in will GENERALLY be filtered in a positive way. Someone could be a complete jerk to me, and I am just over there thinking that person must be going through a rough time and I move on. I am able to let it go easier, and not take it to heart. I've noticed too often that when we experience abuse in any form, but primarily emotional, we aren't giving ourselves time to HEAL after getting away from it. There could be a million reasons why we aren't fully healing, but the point is our life filter becomes skewed as a result. It doesn't necessarily have to be drastic or major abuse either. Our experience with intimate relationships take a toll on our self-image, and it's really important to take the proper and healthy steps to truly heal after being involved in toxic relationships of any form. Instead I see so many of us internalizing and suppressing what we've gone through. SIDE NOTE: dealing with emotional stuff is important, and it doesn't have to be crazy intense, but it does need to be handled and DEALT with! UMMM don't believe me, look around at the world we live in. Mental/emotional health has really fallen short over the years, and there is no valid reason for it other than we DON'T LIKE dealing with emotional type stuff. I digress...

As I Am: Accepting Myself in an Unacceptable Society

I read an article that said true guilt "comes from a lack of internal integrity," and that it was true guilt when we didn't follow our own truth. [Site web article: https://lifecoachonthego.com/how-to-tell-the-difference-between-true-and-false-guilt/]

When we believe (this is important when we talk about VALUES & BELIEFS) something is wrong, and we do it anyway then we feel true guilt. I will pick on something not so heavy as an example. I personally do not like littering. I am not some overzealous environmentalist or anything, but I would rather have nasty sticky trash in my vehicle or even in my own pocket or purse, than throw it outside on the ground. My son can throw a gum wrapper out the car window and not think twice.

Occasionally he will attempt to put it in a trash can but miss only to leave it on the ground next to the trash can. For reasons beyond my understanding, other than he is young, it doesn't bother him at all. I, on the other hand, will miss a trash can and feel so guilty that I will go back and pick up the trash. I even find myself picking up trash when I am in places simply because I just feel like there is no reason I cannot bend over and pick it up to properly dispose of it; and I know it doesn't bother others, so it will stay there and I will feel true guilt if I do not at least pick up a fair amount of trash in public places if I notice it.

Another common example - when you know it is not nice to call someone names, but you do it anyway to fit in. Later you feel terrible because you believe that it is wrong, and you still did it. That is true guilt. True guilt is healthy because it leads us to learn and keeps us accountable for our actions. If we are accountable, we are less likely to go around aimlessly doing whatever, just violently spilling venom because we never feel remorse. True guilt is different than false guilt and serves a healthy purpose even in the world of accepting yourself. Here's the thing, when you are learning to accept yourself as you are in the present moment, you have to evaluate your own beliefs and values.

As you write out your lists, you are going to find out that there are things you believe, but do not yet value as much. This causes us to miss the mark often, and therefore we will feel guilty about that. The thing is you have to know that if it pertains to something you truly do value, then feeling the guilt will help you work towards no longer falling short in that area. For example, I believe in life balance - healthy living physically, mentally, emotionally, and spiritually. I value my health; however, this is an area I have to sit down and actually evaluate. You see when I eat fast food and neglect physical exercise on a regular basis, that does not show that I actually value what I believe in. If I did, I would feel more remorse and true guilt which would lead me to take more conscious steps in the direction to change this.

False guilt is a learned response and is driven by external factors. Generally speaking we feel false guilt when we are approval junkies, people pleasers who constantly think "What will they think about me now?" I read that false guilt is self-abuse, and it's about blaming ourselves for stuff. False guilt connects with fear, false evidence appearing real. We fear rejection of others, we fear that if we do something the wrong way or say the wrong thing then those around us will stop liking us. We fear that if we do not do all these millions of things to keep those around us pleased or those we look up to happy with us, then they will reject us, or worse - shun us. Most of the time these people do not even realize that we are constantly doing things out of our own false guilt, so when the day comes and we snap, they are totally unaware of why. False guilt causes us to live fake lives because we are doing things to make others happy or whatever the reason behind it, and it is denying ourselves of our true thoughts, feelings, and of just being. I also want to insert here, remember several paragraphs above when I first began to discuss guilt? Remember how I talked about the filter people perceive the world around them with? This is a good reminder that so often that filter stemmed from self-imposed insecurities out of our internal fear of rejection, or not fitting in with others. So often the filter we view the world outside of us, comes from a place of our own imposed fears and assumptions. It isn't even always from past hurts or abuse, although it can be, of course. But I learned many times I myself had all these false guilt driven ideas and expectations that filtered how I perceived everything going on around me that I did or did not do. And to my demise I would find myself checking my own thoughts, beliefs, and opinions against those false expectations, and false guilt. I would think if I didn't do this or say that, this other person would be disappointed or mad with me. I thought, "This person expects 'xyz' of me and if I don't live up to THAT, I will no longer have their love and definitely not their acceptance." IT was my filter that I created out of my fears, and the funny thing was that most of the things were completely ridiculous. I won't sugar coat anything either though. There were times I was right in what I thought other people were thinking about me. I stand today knowing people I once thought loved me unconditionally do not. AND THAT'S OKAY!!!!!! People I considered family and friends have incorrectly judged me because I didn't follow their false expectations for me, and THAT IS ALSO OKAY. In that overcompensating, I begin to act in ways very contrary to what I truly believe, think, and even feel guilt of true and false kind. I was hurt when I came to realize that, but I forgive them. I forgive and I remember that they are on their own journey, and I hope they one day learn to unpack their own internal false realities for themselves as I have. I have to work daily to forgive and not allow myself to become bitter. People simply operate out of their inner fears and often do not recognize that for exactly what it is.

So go back to the domino analogy (yes, I am going way back). See how denial is where it all begins? If I am denying that I talk too much, I am going to act in ways to overcompensate for that because I have to prove that what I am denying isn't true. In that overcompensating, I begin to act in ways very contrary to what I truly believe, think, and even feel. Keep adding the dominoes because when you start off denying one thing that you think is not a big deal, that leads to you acting in ways that go against your inner thoughts and feelings; which causes you to not only question yourself, but also makes you feel like a "fake" person. THEN you begin to feel resentment or anger towards the people who told you that you talked too much to begin with; and really, I could keep going on with negative pathways that all come from the first issue of denial!

I'm seriously worn out already just trying to put it all into words for you. But I hope you can see the picture I am desperately trying to paint. This is how we "lose ourselves" so to speak. Many of us never actually found ourselves when we transitioned to young adulthood from the teen years, and therefore I believe this book is going to be so epic. I have worked with teens since I was barely out of my own teen years and I am now 36. Our technology infused society is obsessed with reality television and fictional identities and our young people are not allowing themselves the chance to find out who they genuinely are.

I have been thinking about this for a long time now. I told you guys I have always been overly fascinated with human behavior and the psychology behind it. I like to identify the roots, and then look for solutions because for me knowing the WHY helps motivate me to the change that brings the answers. I believe more than just young people have misplaced their identity. I think we see this issue in older generations because they were taught their identity was in their work or in their heritage.

I am generalizing here but follow me for a minute. When we associate ourselves as a farmer, a teacher, a homemaker, a blue-collar worker, etc., we use what we THINK those things stand for to then identify ourselves. Where does most of what we think come from? Let me be more specific, where does the majority of what we think about roles, and characteristics of these various roles I listed come from? We aren't born with a data bank description for roles. You don't see a 2-year-old being able to depict that a farmer wears overall because of the weather and nature of farming work. Or that this lady must be a homemaker because she has an apron on while she cooks dinner.

The world around us as we grow up DOES influence what we think; our

parents or main caregivers are usually the prime contributor. Then there are our family members, environment, our classmates, and television if we are honest. Alright, now we have the rise in technology, and the rise in single parent homes or even 2 parent homes that are working more and at home less; let's get REAL again for a minute. Lots of false realities playing into the influence of ALL OUR LIVES. Let's say that to some degree, television and social media of all forms have probably contributed to the way we think and process information more than many of us would like to ever admit. And what is on television and all-over social media? False realities, lies, scripted lives that claim to be real, along with fabricated images of what beauty, success, and family should be.

You go to the grocery stores and besides candy, what do you see covering the checkout aisles? Magazine after magazine of false information, false pictures, lies, lies, and more lies! I mean from soap operas of the 80's, the sitcoms over the years, reality shows, and even now we have "survival" shows - and it's all FABRICATED and SCRIPTED! Every bit of it is telling people of all ages who they should be, what they should be doing, thinking, wearing, saying, looking like, believing, feeling, and heck even when they should be using the dang bathroom!!!!

I am going to get on some toes here and pick on my beloved "Christians" and say do not think because many of you once hid from TV, movies, and "secular entertainment" that you were not nearly as affected. It is a lie

if you truly believe that, because I can tell you the same things at work in the secular world was also within your hidden little lives. I mean no disrespect either, I am just telling you from my heart.

How many of you were told by people you looked up to that this type of dress was a sin, that cutting your hair was against the Bible, or whatever it was. I mean I could get very detailed here because I went to a Pentecostal Church and heard so many stories from older generations. But think about it, it was the same underlying force at work. Might have come out very differently, but it made many believe that certain jobs/clothing were for men and others for women, and that various activities were "manly" or "girly". It made many believe activities that were not at all sexual or about sexuality were so because of what? The current advertisement wanted to use that as a selling point.

My argument is that if you think you do not give into marketing and advertisement and that it appalls you, please be aware we are ALL affected to some level. There are so many contributing factors that put these false expectations or false guilt within our thoughts. Not a one of us is exempt. We all have to become aware of how things seep into our subconscious. It's no wonder we are walking around lost as heck, not able to accept ourselves, not able to love who we are.

We don't know WHO THE HECK WE ARE!!!!!!!!!!!

We don't know if we believe this, because if we do then this person over here will think less of us, and maybe even stop being our close friend. Worse, they might even stop loving us. And even more because THEY think whatever it is, they think then we will question if we are "good enough", or if there is something wrong with us because our beliefs or whatever are different from those we respect and love. It is A MESS. And I see it EVERY SINGLE DAY way more than I believe people will openly admit.

Knowing ones-self has become an artifact in this country in my opinion. Now, don't get your panties in a tangle (and where did that saying even come from? I don't know but it is fun to say!). I realize there are probably thousands out there who truly do know themselves, and actually love themselves. There are people who take the time to do this. I UNDERSTAND THAT for those getting defensive. I am only making observations and I am sharing with you what I have seen over the years in my life journey. I am SHARING with you from my perspective, and my personal experiences.

I thought I had found myself folks, well I thought I KNEW who I was. I laugh now because truth is, I was just as blinded as many others are and I know this now because HINDSIGHT, OF COURSE LOL. I know this now because of how I fell apart when life shifted from what I had known, to something extremely different. I know this now when I look at how incredibly worried, I would get over my every move in life, and how I walked around constantly defending myself when it wasn't needed. Sure it's easy to say, "Well eff that, why the heck did you do that mess?" BECAUSE I WAS NOT AWARE OF WHO I WAS THEREFORE I HAD TO UPKEEP WITH SOME FALSE IMAGE I THOUGHT OTHERS HAD OF ME. I HAD TO LIVE UP TO SOME FAKE STANDARDS OF WHAT WAS "SUPPOSE TO BE" SO THAT THOSE I RESPECTED WOULD DEEM ME EQUALLY RESPECTABLE. I WAS AFRAID OF BEING LESS THAN I ACTUALLY WAS BECAUSE I DID NOT KNOW MY OWN WORTH OR VALUE.

This is a layered process in our lives. I believe looking back, that being a young teen mom I did not find myself during the years I was "supposed to." You see this is one of the reasons parents don't want their children doing things like having sex at young ages, well one of the many reasons, but I am not trying to discuss THAT topic here. It will be in another book. But seriously, young adulthood years are meant to be the time we explore life. We challenge what our parents raised us believing, and we are supposed to figure out what it is that WE as individuals value and believe. It's time for mistakes yes, but at the same time it's important not to let those "mistakes" define you... I have noticed that we live in a culture that has become very difficult to not do...

At the end of each and every day we must take inventory of our inner selves. We must ask ourselves if we are dealing with anxiety or depression or stress that is from a place falsely imposed OORRR if there is genuine remorse to be addressed. For us to do that in the healthiest manner, we must be able to truly understand the difference between false guilt and true guilt along with knowing our values and beliefs. Before we dig into that, let's look a little more at how guilt turns into shame causing us to continue in or jump back onto the denial train... Keep in mind that domino analogy too!

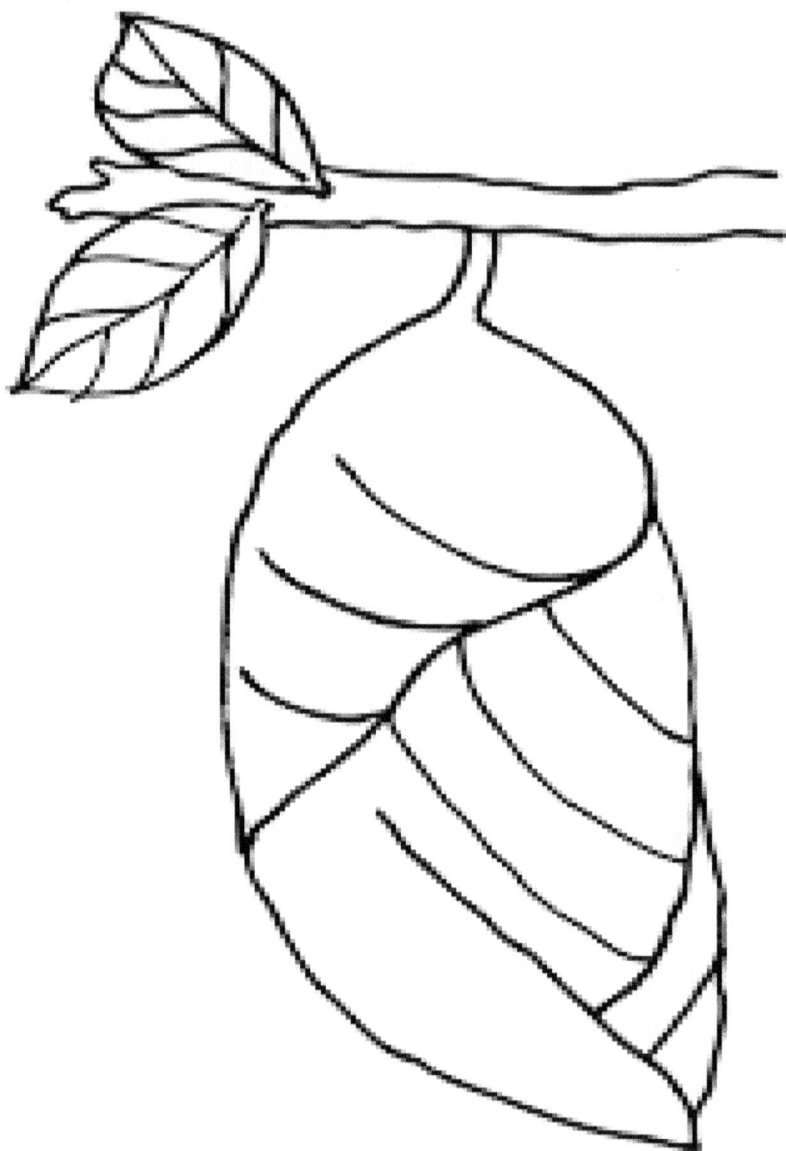

As I Am: Accepting Myself in an Unacceptable Society

Still marinating and working to get rid of what will not fit our new life as a butterfly!

Okay so when I think of shame, I think of something that comes along after I have carried guilt for a long period of time without dealing with it. To me shame is what I feel after I have just covered guilt with denial or flat ignoring it. Webster's dictionary says shame is a painful emotion caused by consciousness of guilt, shortcoming, or impropriety. It also says something that brings censure or reproach; also something to be regretted. (For those wondering, impropriety means rude or immoral behavior: improper behavior or rude or improper quality) …

In my head though, I might feel guilty about littering, but I don't exactly feel ashamed if I do that. For me feeling shame carries a much heavier weight within myself. I felt shame for years over not paying my bills on time because to me that was an area I should have VALUED as more important than I did. Being a single mother who did not get a solid career before having a child was a valid excuse to not be able to pay certain things on time. PRETTY SURE food and other bills (like RENT and ELECTRICITY LOL) took precedent. However, because I would deny the fact that I actually had no idea how to properly budget, I would use being a single young mom as an excuse. It may have been valid to an extent, but the bottom line is - it was still an excuse. I could have taken the time to listen and get financial help.

I recognized more recently that I allowed this to become an area that defined me. I allowed the shame of knowing better, but not doing better keep me captive, along with keeping me in a stuck cycle of financial mess! Worse, it became a cycle and pattern that kept showing up and showing out in my life. The story about my life I believed was defined by this shame and vicious cycle. Without realizing it, I accepted the patterns of this financial roller coaster. In doing so I subconsciously had to live out that story I believed deep within myself (remember back to early in the book where I mentioned what is the story we believe about our lives and ourselves).

My denial and excuses were ways I just put a band-aid over the guilt I originally felt for poor planning. After years it turned into shame causing me to be embarrassed so much so that I actually believed I didn't deserve a partner in life that had better financial habits than myself, so I gravitated to those with habits worse than mine generally. Why is that?? OH YEA I

wanted to feel better about my deep-down hidden shame and guilt. I wanted to remember that I was NOT THAT BAD...(there's that self judgement thing I mentioned early on too). Financial struggles DOES NOT MAKE US BAD people. Shaking my head, but see how the thinking goes?

Writing this openly makes me feel currently like a much more selfish and petty person than I had ever wanted to believe I was, but at the same time I feel empowered too. Empowered because I see how my fear of rejection from society's standards in this area can no longer have such a tight hold on me since I have become aware AND spoke the truth about it.

Like I mentioned in the denial discussion, when you openly confess something you are taking some of its power away. You are no longer hiding or avoiding that thing which is what adds the darkness to it. When we avoid something or hide from it, it's like taking the light from it. When you take away the light you are left with its opposite; darkness.

Out of sight, out of mind is what I think of, and that is yet another lie we too often tell ourselves. All it does is cause that darkness to grow. I remember years ago I got a speeding ticket on my way home from class. I was probably 19 or 20 because my son was still in diapers. Now for some crazy reason I thought if I never paid this ticket, it would just magically be forgotten about. HA.

People I know how ignorant that sounds, and I feel like I was not that unintelligent by any means, but I did not want to face the ticket because I had "no money" to pay something extra! I am sure a year went by if not longer and I never had a single repercussion. I thought I was golden!! I mean I HAD completely forgotten about it. Then one day I was driving my father to a doctor's appointment with my young son with us, and I did not get over out of the passing lane only side. Sure enough there was a cop who proceeded to pull me over. I was informed I had a warrant out for my arrest from failure to take care of that ticket! Lucky for me I was not physically arrested in front of my son because I had metal rods exiting my wrist from a surgery, and my father was not able to drive at the time (this is also another really great thing about living in a small town when raising my son; they often understood things like this annnnnd I knew everyone LOL) The police allowed me to drive us to the station, and then booked me in the county jail. I was there for only 4 hours, but it was very much not magically forgotten just because I did not remember it. It did not go away simply because I kept it hidden from the light....

Let me say that the years raising my son I spent a lot of time being so dad-gum forgetful. It wasn't something I did intentionally ever, and trust me without even recognizing it, I carried this sense of victim mentality because I used so many excuses to justify my actions. This was the story of my life, and this led me to a life lived in shame. I still to this day battle the residue of this, but now I can at least call it out. I can remind myself I have no reason to feel negatively, that it's all a lie. Thing was, I was guilty of sincerely not fully knowing how or where to begin with budgeting or learning how to "adult" in healthy productive ways. I felt ashamed of myself because instead of allowing someone to help me figure out where my behaviors were rooted, I would just find another "reason" to explain why what I did was valid. I say reason, but it was always just another excuse.

Because of this, to me guilt and shame tend to be grouped together, and the issue with that is we have a very ugly taste about feeling shame. So then we associate that with also feeling guilt, and then in turn we gain a very skewed perspective of actual true guilt that should be leading us to repentance. Repenting is simply turning yourself around and away from whatever it is. It is deciding to go the opposite way you are going. When we associate guilt with shame like this, we are then making room for ourselves to create more excuses. We are allowing ourselves to add more dominos to that stack we talked about...

Guilt, true remorse for our actions or choices, can push us forward in positive ways. False guilt leads us to add layers upon layers of undesirable characteristics that cause us to feel shameful for existing. We must learn how to redefine these pictures in our minds eye. If you really desire true self-acceptance, you have to dig these core things out and see them in the true light they are meant to carry. Truth is this, we all should feel true guilt from time to time. We should not feel so poorly about it that we spiral negatively from it though. People close to us should be able to share with us things we need to work on in loving ways; that's just growth.

What I have observed more and more is that because this is viewed in such a twisted or polarized way, people cannot seem to handle constructive criticism. It's as if anything pointed out to them instantly means they are some horrible spawn of Satan or something. I believe this is partially because of this skewed view between the words, and of course there are other contributing factors. But we could start by redefining the words properly.

Guilt and shame are not interchangeable words. False guilt is also a real thing that we need to learn how to identify. We must become more aware of the words we use and think. They truly are life and death, blessings and curses. Webster says the word 'ashamed' means feeling inferior or unworthy. "Guilt is a bad feeling caused by knowing or thinking that you have done something bad or wrong," says Webster. Does that help make the significant difference between the words a little easier to comprehend? We are going to make mistakes. We are going to do things that are not always pleasant or "good". We are going to act out from time to time. Part of the human experience is that we are not perfect in our behaviors or actions all the time. It's part of our life journey, and when we can get back to the place where we remember this, we will see less offended people. I believe.

I truly feel that society would benefit tremendously by redefining several words often used. It feels like time that we take collective action to bring some balance back to the world we live in. Guilt and shame are not meant to define us, and when we can understand this, we can begin to release ourselves from so much unnecessary suffering.

"Shame is a focus on self, guilt is a focus on behavior. Shame is "I am bad." Guilt is "I did something bad." How many of you, if you did something that was hurtful to me, would be willing to say, "I'm sorry. I made a mistake?" How many of you would be willing to say that? Guilt: I'm sorry. I made a mistake. Shame: I'm sorry. I am a mistake."

-Brene Brown-

https://fs.blog/2014/10/brene-brown-guilt-shame/]

As I Am: Accepting Myself in an Unacceptable Society

This is so profound to me. Behavior has room for improvement because we are living in a hurting world, with hurting people. It's okay that behaviors make us feel remorse and are even pointed out to us as being hurtful to others when appropriate. We are not defined by our actions. At least we should not be, and we do have THE CHOICE to not allow ourselves to be defined by them! Shame focuses on self. Shame, however, tells us, "I am bad". That just isn't true. You always have a choice. A choice to get help for areas you need to work on. A choice to take steps that will create new behaviors. A choice to repent, or turn around, from behaviors that are not serving you, or even ones that are flat out toxic and unhealthy. Because we have that choice, I believe that even those who make poor choices creating a series of poor behaviors STILL are not poor or bad people. At the same time I do agree that what I would consider a "good or bad" person is going to differ from what you would say. However, I am learning that I don't like using those words to categorize or label people.

EVEN THE ONES who live lives full of lies, deceit and abusive behaviors. The more I grow and learn about God and myself, the more I see those people as Jesus saw those crucifying Him. I believe it is history that Jesus was a real man, and He really died on a cross. Therefore, it was

real that he said while hanging on that cross, "Father, FORGIVE THEM. THEY DON'T KNOW WHAT THEY DO."

You see, when we are hurt - we lash out. Every single one of us is raised differently. Different traditions, beliefs, morals, and every one of us experiences life in very different ways. We all interpret circumstances through various filters. Some of us are more critical, while others are more gracious. Thing is, for many of us what we know and think is "okay and right" to us, even when it may not be to others. I do believe there are some basic principles we should all live by, but the reality (truth) is that isn't exactly what we see. And remembering that for the MAJORITY of people, they do not actually intentionally do stupid shhh...I mean, stuff!

I realize there are those who do, and well I am not talking about them. I am talking about that person at the grocery store who just lost their spouse and their family lives in other states. They just lost their spouse, who was the breadwinner, but did not have a life insurance policy. They just lost their spouse, and their support system had to leave so they are forced to continue life while not being ready yet. We all process grief differently. I am talking about the single parent who is working 2 jobs to put food on the table, while also trying to keep the electricity on at home, all while trying to still spend quality time with their children. Their children that need extra attention because only 1 parent is around - for whatever reason. That single parent who is also trying to raise these children to make better choices than them in their life. I am talking about the person who gets picked on from every single support person in their life, and they might think that's normal, acceptable behavior. I am talking about the people who have just experienced unexpected health issues, lost their only family vehicle, and just had a crappy time in their life for reasons out of their control.

Some people do not have strong coping skills or any support systems. I am talking about the people we encounter who are hateful or snappy or just plum rude. I am talking about the people who have experienced pain and hurt, and do not realize that they are lashing out. I am talking about people around us that we forget have their own struggles, trials, and lives that, like ours, are never what they seem to be from the outside looking in. I am talking about all of us! We all have bad days. Days where we feel inadequate for our loved ones.

We all have seasons in our life that it seems to just be one constant hard circumstance after another. Seasons when our body chemicals are off, our bodies feel more stress than we recognize. Seasons when we just feel like snapping at people who look at us sideways, or even that we simply think do. I am learning to remind myself most of the time people do not realize how miserable they are behaving, and they honestly do not know what they are doing. I am learning that people do not have the same thought process as me, they cannot read my mind, and they do not pick up the same context clues I do. I am learning to remember that people are living much differently than me.

That might sound like "DUH! But thank you Captain Obvious." But seriously - how many times do we forget? How often do we just assume others think or believe as we do? Even people with whom we have much in common with have so many things different and yet we still have the tendency to not view them outside our limited outlook.

Something so simple while being so stinking complex.

Values & Beliefs

It all comes down to a couple of words that too often are used interchangeably or in connection with each other when they should not be. It's amazing to me how just like guilt and shame tend to be interchangeable so do values and beliefs. As I have researched and looked into these words, I realized that the false identity I was giving them was actually part of the biggest, deepest roots within myself blocking me from the most intimate authentic acceptance of myself. You see I wrote this book for myself just as much as I wrote it for all of you. I will say it a million times over, if I wrote this book and it only changes me then it was still worth every ounce of energy (and every dime) I put into it...

Recognizing that guilt and shame were not interchangeable, and so much of the shame I carried (or even still struggle with) was out of a place of layered false guilt helped me just let that stuff go. Like seriously. I was able to just take a slow, deep breath, and exhale years of unwarranted

shame. In doing that, it was clear to me that next- I had to take these other 2 words that I believed shaped who I was and define them also separately... Values and beliefs.

I researched the definitions to several key words for this book, and I must say as I review my notes, I just am amazed at what I found. I picked up some good stuff during my zillion years of trying to get my college degree, and a website I fell in love with was called Barrett Values Centre.

[https://www.valuescentre.com/mapping-values/values/values-vs-beliefs]

I just get so excited when I read how others can sum up my thoughts in a few powerful sentences. I got that on this site for my words values and beliefs. I must quote their given definitions:

"Beliefs are assumptions we hold to be true. When we use our beliefs to make decisions, we are assuming the causal relationships of the past, which led to the belief, will also apply in the future. In a rapidly changing world where complexity is increasing day by day, using information from the past to make decisions about the future may not be the best way to support us in meeting our needs. Beliefs are contextual: They arise from learned experiences, resulting from the cultural and environmental situations we have faced."

"Values are not based on information from the past and they are not contextual. Values are universal. Values transcend contexts because they are based on what is important to us: They arise from the experience of being human. Values are intimately related to our needs: Whatever we need— whatever is important to us or what is missing from our lives— is what we value.

As our life conditions change, and as we mature and grow in our psychological development, our value priorities change. When we use our values to make decisions, we focus on what is important to us— what we need to feel a sense of well-being."

Now I don't care who you are, THAT is some good stuff. I forgot how perfectly this defined 2 life changing words. I say life changing because as we unfold these descriptions versus what many of us think about when we initially hear them there is no way you will walk away without being challenged to reevaluate. Alright, well that's it. These explanations will be enough! I will just go ahead and tell you THE END! BOOK DROP! (You know instead of mic drop. What? I laughed) ...

JUST JOKING, and I imagine by this part of the book you have come to know me slightly better than that. I truly admire that others can say concisely what I cannot, but let's face it many of us need the whole digging into the deep parts of what's summed up neatly in less wording. For me it helps the concept stick better. Here is where the rubber meets the road you guys. Creating this entire book has challenged me, but it was when I took this section apart that I noticed such a significant shift in how I thought, felt, and spoke about myself. It was when I realized how much of my life that I lived according to beliefs that were not aligned with my values. I will be honest this was really enlightening while also being sad...

I still find myself sitting down with my journal to evaluate what I believe verse what my true values are. Truth is, I do not think its mastery we should expect though. To me it was and continues to be about my personal inner peace. It's my journey to first find out who it is I am, and then accept wholly all of that. Through that full acceptance I found I can then see why God loves me and why, even more than I THINK. It was through that raw, unedited, unmasked acceptance that I was able to see myself as my parents always saw me, and as I see my child... With unconditional love. True love that doesn't depend on my right or wrongs, or the good or bad I do. True love that tells me I am worth all the things I could only dream of before. Things like respect, being treated with dignity, and so much of the words Jesus spoke to his disciples began to be crystal clear. Let's go finish the beginning of this journey....

"Beliefs are assumptions we hold to be true. When we use our beliefs to make decisions, we are assuming the causal relationships of the past, which led to the belief, will also apply in the future. In a rapidly changing world where complexity is increasing day by day, using information from the past to make decisions about the future may not be the best way to support us in meeting our needs.

As I Am: Accepting Myself in an Unacceptable Society

Beliefs are contextual: They arise from learned experiences, resulting from the cultural and environmental situations we have faced."

[https://www.valuescentre.com/mapping-values/values/values-Vs-belefs]

I just have to say," WOW!" I remember one of my pastors told me that, "Our belief system is what we know to be true. And our value system is what we do. Therefore, if the two do not align, I would question if you really believe the said belief system you claim to." I must tell you that even as I write this out his words take on a new understanding to me. I always remember thinking what he said was great stuff, and it impacted me greatly for the good. However, I now see more clearly why there is so much judgment, and self-condemnation among Christians and so much misunderstanding of communication in general.... I want to say I am not picking on Christians; it is just a group of people with common religious or spiritual beliefs and values that I most closely relate with. It's obvious to me now where the root of so much negative comes from without most ever realizing it! Hang with me if you are of a different "religious background", I promise the example will benefit all creeds.

As I Am: Accepting Myself in an Unacceptable Society

If beliefs are assumptions we know to be true, and they are contextual arising from learned experiences, then it's no wonder beliefs change with the times... Therefore, yes what worked for "old timers" in any religion or political party even will not be true for younger timers or whatever group that has differences. I feel like this should solve world wars people!

Think about it... Using the topic of Christians, I can hold the same values as another Christian; I believe Jesus was the son of God who lived and died so that I can be set free from sin. I can value treating others with love, and Jesus teaches us that through the Bible. Those values are the core but depending on the culture and environment of the Christians who I am around and teach me about Christianity the beliefs will differ from other Christians! IT JUST MEANS THAT MY BELIEF SYSTEM IS GOING TO BE DIFFERENT FROM OTHERS!!!!!!!!!!!!!!! DO YOU GUYS GET THE DEPTH OF THAT? Can you see how this correlates to so many things?

Beliefs are passed down! They are the traditions, rituals, the revelations and life experiences someone else had and they taught those around them. It's our family's heritage that we sometimes adopt or discard totally if we do not agree with it. However, it does not mean that the values are not still there!!!!!!!!!!!!!! It just has a different belief attached to it.... (this seriously made my mind explode).

It's just like when you hear someone tell you they value honesty, yet they are very dishonest when it comes to either business matters or some areas in their lives. Usually when you hear a person say, "I am honest, but this isn't really lying. It's just a white lie." Now that doesn't mean they don't value honesty; it just means in that area they were taught a different belief. They have a contextual understanding that the thing isn't lying in a way that hurts others therefore to them the belief doesn't reflect what they value. Because you see the belief, they have about what being honest is - it differs from what they value which may be taking care of their families or whatever.

The main point to get from this is that it is not fair for us to use the beliefs of others as what defines their values, because we may not actually know what their belief is on a particular topic, and it is not productive to ASSUME that just because they are like us in what they value that they are also like us in their beliefs! Beliefs will vary from family to family, city to city, culture to culture! Beliefs are ASSUMPTIONS we hold to be true!

AHH...THAT ALSO MEANS THEY MAY NOT EVEN BE TRUE!!!!!!!!!!!!!!

Going back to my pastor's statement, it wasn't wrong or bad or anything, it just made me realize more how we misinterpret others which leads to the constant bickering among one another within groups that share commonalities. Beliefs are going to be shaped out of various factors, and it's okay for them to change as we do. I think what the significant takeaway is to really know what it is that YOU believe, and why. Then what is it you value and why. I also feel it's important when we are interacting with others, we keep in mind this very thing - IT IS NOT PRODUCTIVE TO ASSUME SOMEONE THAT VALUES WHAT YOU DO ALSO BELIEVES AS YOU.

I work on not assuming anything these days honestly, but truth is along the journey of self-acceptance; we need to practice that internally before we can ever offer the same externally. I will say this again, how we view and subconsciously view ourselves, and how we accept and love ourselves is ultimately what we give to others. We wonder why the world is so dark and full of bitter hateful people; the world is full of people who have lost themselves or never found themselves to begin with. The world is full of those who do not FULLY ACCEPT OR UNDERSTAND HOW TO UNCONDITIONALLY LOVE THEMSELVES! We don't know what it is we believe so we just jump on any bandwagon passing us by. It is not always because they just want to fit in, often they were never shown HOW to figure out what it is that they actually believe!

"Values are not based on information from the past and they are not contextual. Values are universal. Values transcend contexts because they are based on what is important to us: They arise from the experience of being human.

Values are intimately related to our needs: Whatever we need— whatever is important to us or what is missing from our lives—is what we value. As our life conditions change, and as we mature and grow in our psychological development, our value priorities change. When we use our values to make decisions, we focus on what is important to us—what we need to feel a sense of well-being."

[https://www.valuescentre.com/mapping-values/values/values-vs-beliefs]

What we value will change as we grow and mature to certain degrees. However, I personally think something we miss when raising our children (again this is a general observation and I always include myself in whatever I am saying in a general sense) is that we don't teach them to value themselves as clearly as we could. I think this happens without noticing because many of us do not first truly value ourselves individually. One of the things I learned from raising my son and being around so many close friends during the years they raised their babies was that the kids learn more from what they SEE us do as their parents.

My pastor that I mentioned before would tell us, "We teach what we know, but we produce who we are." That really is such truth for the majority. Now like all things I realize and understand that a child can be raised with abusive parents and grow up to be the opposite of that. Even in that though, there will be tendencies and traits that are embedded in the grown child. Unfortunately it usually tends to be the lack of healthy coping skills that will be reproduced, even if the kid grows up to be very different from the parents. The thing is, abusive people are deep down very hurt people that never learned how to feed the right inner voice. Now, before you get upset with me for that know I am not excusing an abusive person's behaviors. I am just saying, when we are raising our children, we are going to produce who we are still even if they make better choices and decide to live a more positive life than the parents. There will still be things produced such as the lack of certain developmental skills. It's hard to show someone around us how to value themselves if we do not understand what that looks like. It is difficult to believe our parents when they tell us as insecure preteens and teens that we are beautiful and worthy of love and acceptance, if they themselves are not walking that out. How does that look? What exactly does that mean? I mean we all know those arrogant, self-absorbed people out there who do not see past the end of their own nose; does valuing myself look like that? Absolutely not. It's this dichotomy; selfishness vs self-love. Self-value, which I believe society and media have completely blurred the two - leading us to walk around in false guilt and shame, dare we choose to value ourselves. In this same thought, I also feel that it's because somewhere along the course of history, we have lost a balance and understanding for personal boundaries, tilting the tendency towards self-absorption. I can't tell you when it happened, but let's take a minute to think about it.

Over the years people have given more and more of themselves to their jobs, families, and friends while neglecting their individual needs. This happens for so many reasons that if I tried to name them, I would need another entire chapter. The demands of trying to survive have left us fighting for any ounce of inner strength or peace. And it is cliché for Christians to just walk around reminding us that true inner peace is found when we know Jesus. Okay so I am not denying that, however, let me add something - knowing Jesus or any other faith belief you have is not some magic you can repeat mentally, hoping one day you understand and feel it to be real. I told you I have been of Christian faith for 18+ years, I was a Bible thumper, church was our refuge and second home. Yet for years I did not have a solid grasp on true inner peace. Period.

As I Am: Accepting Myself in an Unacceptable Society

We often forget there is so much more to just throwing our beliefs at people, and again please do not think my casual or maybe disgruntled tone is me undermining my own faith because it certainly is not. I am simply saying that as human beings, we need more than just a sentence that fills the air when we are unsure of what to say to someone. Self-value is not the same as self-absorbed, and I PRAY reading this book many more will finally wake up and get this. We hear it all the time, if we don't take care of ourselves there will be nothing left to give out to our jobs,

families, and friends. But how many of us take this to heart? How many of us VALUE ourselves enough that this VALUE aligns with our personal beliefs of commitment, loyalty, charity, or whatever else it is in our belief systems that make us feel as if we need to be caring for others? Here is the thing, as parents if we do not understand how to value ourselves, how can we raise future generations to do that? We cannot. Let's look at the current society; I personally think the balance overall is so far one way or another and that is because, as I've said, somewhere the balance became lost. We wanted our children to not struggle or go through what we did so much so that we see entitlement as an epidemic. It's not that the mindset of giving your children a better life is negative, it's that we lost the balance. I really wanted to address the topic of boundaries in this book, but it's more fitting for my next book about patterns; but I have to stress the importance of healthy boundaries in all areas of our lives.

Having a clear understanding of what we value, helps us then be able to define healthy boundaries for ourselves so that we can be sure we aren't walking around on the verge of burnout or mental breakdowns. I REALLY should say so we aren't walking around IN A CONSTANT STATE OF burnout and mental breakdowns.

Again, Values are intimately related to our needs: Whatever we need—whatever is important to us or what is missing from our lives—is what we value. As our life conditions change, and as we mature and grow in our psychological development, our value priorities change. I want to emphasize something from this statement;

As I Am: Accepting Myself in an Unacceptable Society

AS OUR LIFE CONDITIONS CHANGE, AND AS WE MATURE AND GROW IN OUR PSYCHOLOGICAL DEVELOPMENT, OUR VALUE PRIORITIES CHANGE...

This reminded me to reflect to when I was my son's age, 18. What I valued then was different than what I value now. Granted there will always be something that we value all through our lives, but keep in mind what this statement is saying, as our life conditions change...

This is so multi-leveled for me, and honestly, I am having a tough time to present all the information running through my head to you in a way that makes some tangible sense. I would like to start with the individual understanding then I will explain how this can also help us hopefully understand others a little better too, which I believe is another important part of learning how to fully accept and love ourselves. Not a huge role of course, because it must first start within ourselves; but others impact us and for me, understanding more about them has benefited my journey greatly.

Alright so let me note there are going to be some values many of us carry throughout our entire lives. Well, I don't think I can address this yet because the thing is what I was taught to value and what you were taught will differ. I mean, I suppose I could say most people I have value family and health. But then when we look deeper, even that as a standard value seems to be less universal than it should be. WE SHOULD value human lives in general and, we should value someone else's life as we do our own because those people also have or are part of a family just as we are. We SHOULD value life as a gift and a blessing, but sadly I question how strong that value is anymore.

Webster gives the word VALUE several definitions of course: "the monetary worth of something; a fair return or equivalent in goods, services, or money for something exchanged; relative worth, utility, or importance." It gives some more but I chose to list what I think of most when I hear the word. However, I do want to add one just for "food for thought", because I personally have never thought of this definition. Listed as 7a- "relative lightness or darkness of a color: luminosity, b: THE RELATION OF ONE PART IN A PICTURE TO ANOTHER WITH RESPECT TO LIGHTNESS AND DARKNESS..."

As I Am: Accepting Myself in an Unacceptable Society

Go with me here for just a minute and then I will get back on track. So I looked this up as it pertains to color to get a full understanding. The article I found by Charlotte Jirousek says, "Value is an important tool for the designer/artist, in the way that it defines form and creates spatial illusions." It goes on to discuss how contrast value and gradation value create different looks and so on. Okay so let me tie this back to our topic of value, one of the ways we are given "depth" if you will, is also by what we value.

What makes us stand apart from animals, and other living creatures like plants and ocean life? We have higher functioning thought processes with reasoning, values, and beliefs among other things, yes, I understand.

But the point is we are not just instinctual beings. So our values and how we define and understand them are a big chunk of what makes us human beings, it is a contributing factor to our personalities too. Our values are part of our individual tools that help define who we are, what we want to express and be to the world outside of our internal self! To repeat what I said before my rabbit trail, our values can and do change.

As I Am: Accepting Myself in an Unacceptable Society

It's OKAY though! It's because of this information I realized that defining individual value, as in self-value has become something that we have taken for granted, I think. I mean how often do many of us think others don't have any "values" these days, or we say our kids don't value their toys and clothes we spend so much money on because we don't make them earn it like maybe they had to during the Great Depression era. We say the "value" of a dollar is forgotten because people do not get paid according to their actual worth, whether under or overpaid according to their work ethic. So we toss the word around, but have we ever sat and defined to ourselves what it is exactly we value in life? Or how we value our own self-worth?

This is where I will chime in with my Christian beliefs and say that all people are priceless. For me, even if you do not believe in Jesus Christ as I do, or you have a much different belief or even none, I still believe all human life is priceless. My beliefs tell us we are worth the Son of God dying on a cross so that we can be reunited with God while here on this sinful, fallen world. (I promise I am not getting preachy.) Truth is though, even those who believe their lives are priceless, and worth so much more than the lower end of say, payment if you think in terms of monetary value; they do not live as if they truly feel that way. Truth is even Christians lose hope, self- condemn, self-hate, self-isolate, etc. Even the very ones who are supposed to believe that their life is so much more valuable than they ever feel in any moment of hardship, struggle to sincerely understand how to value themselves.

I want to also bring to your awareness while we are here, how the given definition of values can help us understand others better and why that is so important on our own journey. Think about the people you know that took a complete 180 degree turn in their lives. I don't like saying let's say they went from good to bad because that isn't fair to say, in my opinion. I mean obviously I understand some behaviors are just detrimental to the individuals' wellbeing as well as anyone around them, but I am not about making those judgment calls. I am just about helping you look at those people among others that come to mind with new eyes. A different perspective.

Look back at our definition, VALUES ARE INTIMATELY RELATED TO OUR NEEDS. The definition we are using also says AS OUR LIFE CONDITIONS

As I Am: Accepting Myself in an Unacceptable Society

CHANGE... Things in life change all the time. My personal life conditions change like a roller coaster, and I am well aware that isn't the case for everyone, and it may not even be the case for the majority. However, the truth is life conditions still change. People's needs change as that happens. People's needs change as they age too. I won't say grow and mature because often we do not SEE people growing or maturing in our own concept or view of it, so I am just stating what is inevitable without putting anyone down. Also, I need to add that the rate at which others do grow or mature should not be as much of our concern as so many of us make it. I struggle with that myself, and I learned after pushing people I loved away that it is not my job or responsibility to determine the growth or maturity of others. I am only responsible for my own, and to help guide those (as my son) under my authority, if you will, how they can and should want to grow and mature.

Notice I said, "HELP GUIDE," which means still not judge or dictate to them what growth is for them. Thing is this, we never know where people are at in their lives. Can we make educated guesses? Maybe, but I would tell you that we really should not. I just don't believe you can look at a person's actions and determine what they value, or fairly determine that they are being some type of hypocrite even. I remind you that when people's life conditions change, what people need often changes, which means that their values are going to change even if it's not known to them. The last thing they need is us judging their life, or even shunning them because suddenly we think they flew the coop or jumped off the deep end. I go a step further and remind my fellow Christians this is also why so often people get wrongly judged or mistreated by other believers as well as why many get called hypocrites! It's because we do not realize how values can change without people taking actual notice. This is why when people move about life, and a significant event happens, they might go into what society says is a "life crisis" (I don't say midlife one anymore, because I've seen it at all ages.)

It is not beneficial to us as individuals or a society to make assumptions about others based on their actions we see. I bring this to your attention because along your self love and acceptance journey, you have to remind yourself that you really do not know what state others are in internally, nor do you know what kind of conditions their lives are in. Therefore, we cannot take the actions and words of others so personally. This is not telling you to allow yourself to be walked on or abused. This is telling you to simply keep in mind people who are hurting will hurt others. People who are stressed and full of anxiety will project that outwardly, often unmeaning or even unknowingly. In the journey of true self-acceptance and love, we have to first show ourselves the understanding and grace when we go through life changes, so we can THEN offer the same understanding and grace to others. This still does not mean you have to expose yourself constantly to people that are rude or mean, but it means that you just need to take it less personally. It means we have to remember that how they act is not always a reflection of us, it's a reflection of their inner state. They are confused, or lost, or hurt and sadly enough; many choose to live in denial without even knowing it. And yes, even Christians. No one is exempt. Even those of us who have gotten a solid grasp of true self-acceptance and love have their days that aren't as good as others.

When we start to understand what it is we truly value in life, we can understand even more what it is we believe. We have to understand that valuing our own mental, emotional, and physical health should come at the top of our lists. If we value our family, we should want to value ourselves that much more. When we VALUE something or someone, we then take more positive care and actions towards or regarding that thing or person.

We are a whole being, and physical health is talked about regularly, but many of us do not truly value our health or we would all take better care of our physical bodies. Folks I am preaching to myself too! I am making changes myself to take more positive actions for my physical health because I value myself on a whole new level these days. However, we must not forget emotional health is holding hands with mental health and this is another area America for sure is lacking - in how we value or view it. Emotional health has really been sloughed off partially because of technology. You see, it's because of technology we also hear about all the crappy things happening so much in the world. It's because of technology then we get drowned in negative sh~ahem~ STUFF, and that impacts our very being in ways most of us will never see until it's too late. That negativity makes people bitter, angry, fearful, resentful, forces them to live in the past, and I mean the list goes on folks...

It makes us neglect the art of communication with strangers because we walk around scared to death of some kid in a dark hoodie, or we plum forget how to interpret tone in others talking because we text and communicate behind a screen more than face to face or on the phone. I mean, this all contributes to our emotional and mental being. What's even more insane to me is that in turn all that also adds to our physical being, and it adds negatively! The evidence of how all this affects our physical bodies blows my mind! Please take this book seriously. Take what you gain, research for yourself from credible sources, and pass it along. Teach by example, show people how you came to awareness, and how you learned how to authentically accept yourself. Show them how you unraveled your beliefs and values in order to define them and redefine them so that you weren't walking around unhappy without really knowing why.

Show others that they can share the same values or beliefs while still having different ones at the same time. Show them that just because

223

you both value something the same, the beliefs that support can be different. TO me that is true unity. Unity is not conforming. It's coming together during the diversity. It's having the same values yet respecting the belief systems that stand behind them are different. Learn how to value yourself, your whole self.

FINALLY, A BEAUTIFUL BUTTERFLY BREAKS OPEN THE OUTER COVERING AND EMERGES WITH SOFT, PRETTY WINGS

As I Am: Accepting Myself in an Unacceptable Society

I dare to say this is the beginning of the end. I dare to say I hope you read this, and you dig deep. Dig deep into your own areas of denial, the myths you believe, and the lies you bought over the years just because people around you said it was the truth. Dig deep into those areas in your life that keep you feeling guilty and shameful, so that you can really evaluate if you are carrying false guilt; so that you can analyze shame that should never have been such because it falsely imposed upon you. I encourage you to dig into yourself and discover or rediscover who you really are. I challenge you to accept yourself, your whole self, not an ounce more, not an inch less.

Accept the parts of yourself that you don't want to and are difficult for you to do so but KNOW that in doing so you will lose some of the power that makes it much easier for you to chisel those undesirable traits away. I tell you from experience so many times during my journey to accept and love myself as I am, those areas hard to face melted away without much effort after the accepting part. I remind you that at the end of the day, no one can make you act out of the emotions you feel no matter how their actions affect how you feel. You still have the power to not let the actions of others hinder you. You have a choice. You are not responsible for anyone else, only yourself. You are only able to change you. The worlds solution to all the crimes, and hate acts starts with each individual. It starts with you. You make the changes you need to be a better more authentic true self and watch how those around you will follow suit. Then and only then can we see the larger scale change.

As I Am: Accepting Myself in an Unacceptable Society

You make a difference in all you think, say, and do. You speak life or death, good or bad, right or wrong, love or hate. Please, choose love and life. Dig deep about what your journey towards genuine, authentic self-love means for the rest of the world, and generations ahead. Dig deep to find the power to overcome mountains, the strength to up-root any non-serving belief systems that were passed onto you with good meaning. Look within to find God, or whatever your belief is. Everything we need to overcome ANYTHING is all within us. We just have to do the work to find it. I believe God is in our very DNA, and we just have to learn how to tap in. We just must turn the receptors on so that the purest of light can shine completely through us. We just must do a little work to rid ourselves of all the rose-colored glasses we wear unknowing to us. Don't just let the words come out of your mouth that you truly love and accept yourself, PROVE it to YOURSELF. SHOW it to YOURSELF! DIG DEEP!

As I Am

A	B	C	D	E	F	G	H	I	J	K	L	M	N	O	P	Q	R	S	T	U	V	W	X	Y	Z
				14				23	9				3			11									

I _ _ L L _ _ _ _ H O L L _ _ _ _ E _
9   24 4 3 3 8   15 12 22   2 23 11 3 3 8   15 16 16 14 13 1

L L O _ _ E L . _ _ I _ _ . _ H E _ E
15 3 3   11 24   21 8 19 14 3 24   15 19   9   15 21   2 23 14 5 14

I _ _ . H O _ I _ _ .
9   15 21   23 11 2   9   15 21

As I am - I forgive my shortcomings, I accept my flaws, and I embrace my strengths.

As I am - I choose to learn how to be healthy in thought first so that I can be healthy in all other areas of my being.

As I am - I allow myself grace and time to heal from wrongdoings I have done, along with that of others.

As I am - I choose to let go of the things I just cannot change or fix.

As I am - I choose to love myself and accept myself even when those I respect and honor may not.

As I Am: Accepting Myself in an Unacceptable Society

As I am - I commit to not taking others personally so that I live life and not allow it to live me.

As I am - I accept those who do not accept me first because change begins with me.

As I am - I will laugh more than I cry, and I will allow myself to feel emotions I once ran from or self-medicated for, because I am worth living emotionally and mentally free.

As I am - I choose to see myself not through the eyes of social media or society, but through the eyes of my Creator, through the eyes of something greater than my understanding because as I am, I am beautiful...

As I am - I am enough.

As I am - I am worthy of a healthy, abundant, prosperous life.

As I am - I am the change I want to see in the world.

As I Am... I ACCEPT MYSELF!!

AS I AM... I CHOOSE TO LOVE AND VALUE MYSELF!!

With MUCH LOVE,

~ Danielle Alyse ~

References

- ✓ *Braving the Wilderness* by Brene Brown (p40)

- ✓ https://www.everystudent.com/wires/Godreal.html

- ✓ http://coldcasechristianity.com/2015/why-the-information-in-our-dna-points-to-the-existence-of-god/

- ✓ YouTube Channel - **How to ADHD**: *"The Girl Is Great"*

- ✓ *"Tribes"* by Seth Godin (p108)

- ✓ https://www.valuescentre.com/mapping-values/values/values-vs-beliefs

- ✓ http://char.txa.cornell.edu/language/element/color/color.htm

- ✓ *Switch on Your Brain* by Dr. Caroline Leaf

- ✓ *The Four Agreements* by Don Miguel Ruiz

- ✓ YouTube Channel - **Goalcast's**: 10 Topmost Epic Inspirational Speeches.

- ✓ www.goinswriter.com

- ✓ https://www.psychologytoday.com/us/blog/freedom-learn/201402/five-myths-about-young-people-and-social-media

As I Am: Accepting Myself in an Unacceptable Society

About the

Author

"A genuine diamond in the rough", Danielle Alyse is a profound author, motivational speaker and influencer. Her life's obstacles have molded her into a magnificent woman of wisdom, being able to allow others to not only confide in her but receive advice and insight. However, this wisdom did not come without a price, as Danielle contributes much of her wisdom to the obstacles that she has had to overcome herself, including becoming a single teenage mother. It is through her faith in God and creativity that she has flourished into a

woman of positivity and compassion, ready at any call to help others.

Danielle challenges others to see the silver lining in whatever

circumstance that they are facing and believes that love is the answer to

heal any wound. She has a passion to help others live the life that they

dream by helping them to overcome the obstacles that attempt to

sabotage them. Danielle studies psychology and human behavior, has a

long-term career in the medical field, and has raised an exceptional son

- despite their obstacles.

www.ingramcontent.com/pod-product-compliance
Lightning Source LLC
Chambersburg PA
CBHW070030100426
42740CB00013B/2646